Elite • 187

Byzantine Imperial Guardsmen 925–1025

The *Tághmata* and Imperial Guard

RAFFAELE D'AMATO ILLUSTRATED BY GIUSEPPE RAVA
Series editor Martin Windrow

First published in Great Britain in 2012 by Osprey Publishing,
Midland House, West Way, Botley, Oxford, OX2 0PH, UK
43-01 21st Street, Suite 220B, Long Island City, NY 11101, USA
Email: info@ospreypublishing.com

Osprey Publishing is part of the Osprey Group.

© 2012 Osprey Publishing Ltd.

All rights reserved. Apart from any fair dealing for the purpose of private study, research, criticism or review, as permitted under the Copyright, Designs and Patents Act, 1988, no part of this publication may be reproduced, stored in a retrieval system, or transmitted in any form or by any means, electronic, electrical, chemical, mechanical, optical, photocopying, recording or otherwise, without the prior written permission of the copyright owner. Enquiries should be addressed to the Publishers.

A CIP catalogue record for this book is available from the British Library

Print ISBN: 978 1 84908 850 3
PDF ebook ISBN: 978 1 84908 851 0
ePub ebook ISBN: 978 1 78096 887 2

Editor: Martin Windrow
Page layout by: Ken Vail Graphic Design, Cambridge, UK (kvgd.com)
Index by Zoe Ross
Typeset in Sabon and Myriad Pro
Originated by PDQ Media, Bungay, UK
Printed in China through World Print Ltd.

13 14 15 16 17   11 10 9 8 7 6 5 4 3 2

Osprey Publishing is supporting the Woodland Trust, the UK's leading woodland conservation charity, by funding the dedication of trees.

www.ospreypublishing.com

DEDICATION
To my dear friend and brother Taxiarchis Kolias,
with whom this project was born.

ACKNOWLEDGEMENTS
The author would like to thank all the scholars and friends who have helped during the preparation of this book, and the museums and institutes visited.

First I would like to express my gratitude to Prof Taxiarchis Kolias, Director of the Institute for Byzantine Studies in Athens, who has inspired and encouraged this project since 1997. Prof Livio Zerbini of the newly constituted Laboratory of the Danubian Provinces has been fundamental in the obtaining of the necessary permissions for visits and photography. For access to the mainly unpublished material from Bulgaria I am grateful for the kindness of my friend Prof Valeri Yotov of the Archaeological Museum in Varna. My gratitude for their patient efforts in obtaining permissions for me in Turkey goes to my friends Ilkay and Ayca Dost, and also, for his great courtesy, to Dr Zeynep Kiziltan, Director of the Instanbul Archaeological Museum. Thanks also to Prof Vane Sekulov, archaeologist of Strumica Museum, Macedonia; to Father Igoumenos of the Iviron Monastery, Mount Athos; to Dr John Macnamara, Director of the World Museum of Man, Florida; and to the staffs of the Cathedral Museum of St Sophia, Kiev; the Biblioteca Nazionale, Turin; the Regional Museum, Kazanlik, Bulgaria; the Mechitarist Library, Venice; the Deutches Archaeologisches Institut, Rome; and the Gerhard Hirsch Nachfolger, Munich.

A special acknowledgement is due to my illustrator Giuseppe Rava, who has carried out my wishes regarding the colour plates with great patience and passion.

ARTIST'S NOTE
Readers may care to note that the original paintings from which the colour plates in this book were prepared are available for private sale. All reproduction copyright whatsoever is retained by the Publishers. All enquiries should be addressed to:

Giuseppe Rava, via Borgotti 17, 48018 Faenza (RA), Italy
www.g-rava.it
info@g-rava.it

The Publishers regret that they can enter into no correspondence upon this matter.

CONTENTS

INTRODUCTION 4

CHRONOLOGY 5

THE REGIMENTS – FORMATION & ORGANIZATION 10
The Thémata . The Tághmata: *Skhólai – Eskoubitores – 'Víghla' or 'Arithmós' – Ikanátoi – Athanatoi – Noúmeroi* and *Teichistai* . *Vasilikoploimon* (the Constantinople fleet) The Imperial Guard: *Vasilikê Etaireía – Vasilikodhrómonion* (the Imperial flotilla) – *Maghlavítai – Vasilikoi Anthropoi* . Other Guard units: *Archontogennhematai – Sardoi* – the Varangian Guard . Clothing

WEAPONS & EQUIPMENT 41
Weapons: Swords – daggers – spears – maces – axes – bows . Defensive equipment: Helmets – body armour: lamellar, scale and mail – 'soft' armour – shields . Horse equipment

SELECT BIBLIOGRAPHY 61

INDEX 64

BYZANTINE IMPERIAL GUARDSMEN 913–1025
THE *TÁGHMATA* AND IMPERIAL GUARD

INTRODUCTION

Between the 9th and 11th centuries the East Roman Empire, at that time dominating most of south-eastern Europe from its capital in Constantinople, enjoyed a period of unprecedented splendour and renewed vigour under the rule of the Macedonian emperors of the Porphyrogenitus dynasty. (The modern Anglophone convention of referring to this polity as the Byzantine Empire is necessarily followed in this text for the sake of clarity, but it should be remembered that the inhabitants of the Eastern empire called themselves '*Rhomaioi*' or Romans. The Byzantine state derived directly and without interruption from the Eastern capital, administration and provinces of the Late Roman state, which had survived the barbarian invasions of the 4th and 5th centuries AD that destroyed the Western Empire.)

The Macedonian dynasty, originating in north-western Thrace, acceded to the throne of Byzantium due to the energy and intelligence of its founder, Basil I (r.867–886). It based its strength on the twin foundations of a reasoned policy of fiscal and bureaucratic centralization, which allowed the emperors to contain the centrifugal tendencies of the powerful Anatolian aristocracy, and – above all – on military power. Despite the distractions of struggles over the Imperial succession, during this period the army was consistently well organized, well trained and well paid. The proof of its efficiency is the success of the 9th–11th century Byzantine emperors in overcoming the serious crisis caused by Simeon I of Bulgaria's invasion of the Western provinces; in repelling attacks against Constantinople itself by the Russo-Scandinavians of Igor and Svyátoslav of Kiev; and in resisting pressure in the East from powerful Islamic enemies – both the Hamdanid Emirate of Aleppo and Mosul (the guardian and rival of the now-decadent Abbasid Caliphate of Baghdad), and the Fatimids, who from 969 dominated Egypt and threatened Byzantine Syria. The elite element of the armies that achieved this success were the regiments forming the Imperial *Tághmata*, stationed around the capital, and the Guards forming the military elements of the Imperial household.

Nikêphóros II Phokás (r.963–969), Iohannes Dzimiskés (r.969–976) and Basil II Porphyrogenitus (r.976–1025) were the protagonists of the great military victories that characterized the 'age of Byzantine reconquests' spanning the late 10th and early 11th centuries. These triumphs were due not only to the military genius of these rulers, but to the technical and organizational legacy of Imperial Rome. At the time of Basil II's death in 1025 the empire extended from the river Danube to the Euphrates, and from the Adriatic Sea to the mountains of Armenia.

Byzantine sword guard of the 10th or 11th century from Pliska, Bulgaria, with 'sleeve' extension down blade. (Photo courtesy Prof Valeri Yotov)

CHRONOLOGY

(Byzantine victories against external enemies are printed in *italic* type.)

June 913 Costantine VII Porphyrogenitus, seven-year-old son of the *Vasiléfs* (Emperor) Leo VI the Wise, succeeds his uncle Alexander on the Byzantine throne, under the regency of the Patriarch Nicholas the Mystic.

August 913 First siege of Constantinople by the Bulgarian Czar Simeon.

September 914 Simeon conquers Hadrianopolis.

Summer 915 *Forces of a coalition of the Emperor of Byzantium, the dukes of Naples and Gaeta, the Lombard princes of Salerno, Capua and Benevento, and the Pope, destroy the Muslim stronghold at the mouths of the River Garigliano near Capua, Italy.*

August 917 Expedition against the Bulgarians led by Leo Phokás, *Dhoméstikos* of the *Skhólai*, fails with the defeat at Acheloo and new setbacks for the Empire near Catasyrtae; Simeon is left the master of the Balkan peninsula.

September 920 The *Vasiléopator* Rhomanós Lecapênós becomes co-regent of the young Constantine VII and the dominant figure of the Byzantine state.

921 or 922 Battle of Phegai against the Bulgarians; weighed down by his armour and equipment, the *Dhroungários* of the Imperial fleet, Alexis Moselés, is drowned.

924 Second Bulgarian siege of Constantinople. Simeon overthrows the Byzantine-allied Serbian *Zupan* Zacharias; Rhomanós I names his sons to the succession; *victory of the Imperial fleet over the Arabs of Leo of Tripoli near Lemnus.*

May 927 Death of Czar Simeon of Bulgaria; Byzantine influence strengthens throughout the Balkans.

OPPOSITE PAGE
An Imperial Guardsman of c. AD 1000. The *klivanion* corselet is gilded. The skirt of the *roukhon* tunic is grey embroidered with gold crosses, and the gold-patterned border shows flower motifs; the narrow sleeves are light blue with gold dots. The *chlamys* cloak is red, the trousers (*anaxyrida*) are in light blue and light yellow, and the sash is in silver. The spearshaft is gold and black; the small *cheiroskoutarion* shield is scarlet with white ornaments, a silver rim and a gold boss. For a reconstruction, see Plate H2. (*Menologion* of Basil II, folio 215, Biblioteca Apostolica Vaticana, Rome; facsimile by Pio Franchi de Cavalieri, author's collection)

Iron 11th-century Byzantine or Bulgarian sword guard for a single-edged sabre, from Bulgaria. The empire's multi-cultural armies included *Pharganoi* Turkish troops, and Khazars. (Photo courtesy Prof Valeri Yotov)

928 *Erzerum falls into Byzantine hands; raids against the Fatimid Arabs.*

931–934 *Victorious campaigns of Iohannes Kourkoúas, Dhoméstikos of the Skholaí, in Armenia and northern Mesopotamia; conquest of Melitene; Magyar raids are successfully contained.*

September 938 Saif ad-Dawla, the Hamdanid Emir of Mosul and Aleppo, defeats Iohannes Kourkoúas in the Euphrates Valley, compelling the Armenian and Iberian principates to recognize his sovereignty.

June 941 Rus attack on Constantinople; *the Varangian fleet of Prince Igor is destroyed by the Greek Fire of the Imperial warships led by the* Parakoimómenos *Theophanes.*

942–943 *Successful Mesopotamian campaign of Iohannes Kourkoúas against the Hamdanids: reconquest of Martyropolis, Amidas, Daras and Nisibis; siege and successful storming of Edessa. New Magyar raid into the Balkans is repelled.*

September 944 Rhomanós I is deposed by his sons Stephan and Constantine, and exiled for life to a monastery on the island of Prote.

January 945 Arrest and banishment of Rhomanós Lecapenós' sons, leaving Constantine VII as the sole *Avtokrator* (an alternative title to *Vasiléfs* for the emperor).

949 Constantine Gongilas leads unsuccessful expedition against Arab pirate bases on Crete; *conquest of Germanicea along the Euphrates border.*

950 Saif ad-Dawla's 30,000-strong army ravages the regions of Tzamandos and Charsianon, overcoming the *Dhoméstikos* Várdhas Phokás.

26 October 950 *On his way home, Saif ad-Dawla is ambushed and defeated by the* Stratêgós *Leo Phokás in the passes of Darb al Gawzat and Aqabat on the Germanicea front.*

951–952 Seeking to strike a decisive blow against the Emir of Sicily, Constantine VII sends to Calabria (southern Italy) an army commanded by Malakinos and a fleet led by Makroiannes, but on 7 May 952 the army is defeated near Gerace. *Imperial victories in the East against the Hamdanids.*

953 New Arab conquest of Germanicea; Saif ad-Dawla defeats and captures Constantine Phokás, son of the *Dhoméstikos* Várdhas Phokás.

956 *At the head of Thracian and Macedonian troops and contingents of the Imperial fleet, Marianos Argyros,* Patríkios *and* Stratêgós *of Calabria and Lombardy, restores Byzantine authority over Naples and crushes southern*

Italian rebels. Leo Phokás defeats Abu 'Asa'ir, cousin of Saif ad-Dawla, near Duluk.

June 957 Nikêphóros Phokás, son of Várdhas, captures the Syrian city of Hadath.

958 Conquest of Samosata by Iohannes Dzimiskés. The *Stratêgós* Marianos Argyros is defeated by Arab armies in Calabria.

November 959 Death of Constantine VII Porphyrogenitus; his son Rhomanós II succeeds him as sole Emperor of Byzantium.

959–961 Successes against the Magyars. The Dhoméstikos *of the East, Leo Phokás, wins a remarkable victory over Saif ad-Dawla on 9 November 960. Nikêphóros Phokás, the 'White Death of the Saracens', subjugates Crete.*

961–962 *Nikêphóros Phokás leads a victorious campaign against Saif ad-Dawla; after a last successful Muslim raid in Cappadocia, Anazarba, Germanicea, Raban and Doliches are reconquered, and the Hamdanid capital Aleppo is sacked.*

963 *Hungarian invasion of the Balkans; Marianos Argyros, recalled from Italy and elected* Dhoméstikos *of the Western Skhólai, defeats the invaders.*

15 March 963 Premature death of Rhomanós II Porphyrogenitus; his widow Theophanó rules as regent in the name of the two young princes, Basil and Constantine.

August 963 With the complicity of Theophanó, Nikêphóros Phokás takes Imperial power.

Autumn 963 *Iohannes Dzimiskés wins a victory over the Cylician Saracens at the 'Bloody Hill'.*

965 *The strongholds of Tharsus and Mopsuestia are overcome; the Imperial fleet regains control of Cyprus; new military operations in Calabria and Sicily, near Rometta and Demenna; defeat of the Imperial fleet in the Strait of Messina.*

966–968 *Emperor Nikêphóros Phokás leads a successful expedition into Syria.*

28 October 969 *The* Stratêgói *Phokás and Burtzes regain possession of Antioch in Syria; capitulation of Aleppo, and establishment of the Byzantine* Théma *of Syria.*

December 969 Conspiracy of Iohannes Dzimiskés and Theophanó; Nikêphóros Phokás is murdered in his bed, and Dzimiskés is crowned *Vasiléfs* in the church of St Sophia.

970–971 Russian-Bulgarian alliance against the Empire, led by Prince Svyátoslav of Kiev; the *Magistrós* Várdhas Phokás, nephew of Nikêphóros, moves against Dzimiskés.

April–July 971 *Iohannes Dzimiskés takes Preslav, the Bulgarian capital; siege of Silistra; Prince Svyátoslav capitulates; Czar Boris of Bulgaria is captured and taken to Constantinople.* The Egyptian Fatimids threaten Antioch.

972 *Iohannes Dzimiskés advances in Mesopotamia.*

974–975 *Byzantine offensive in Syria and Palestine: conquest of Baalbek, Damascus, Tiberias, Nazareth and Acre, and assault and capture of Caesarea; Emperor Iohannes Dzimiskés gets within 18 miles (30km) of Jerusalem.* New insurrection against the central power by the *Magistrós* Várdhas Phokás is subdued by the young Co-Emperor Basil.

Helmet from Ozana. The dating is debatable; some scholars believe it is a modified 14th-century bascinet, but the traces of a particular kind of nasal protection, and comparison with 11th-century miniatures, could support an earlier Byzantine origin. (Kazanlik Regional Museum; author's photo)

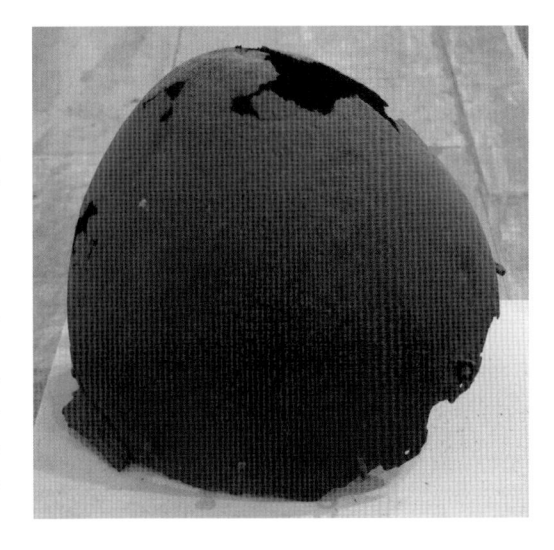

THEMES AT BASIL II's DEATH, 1025

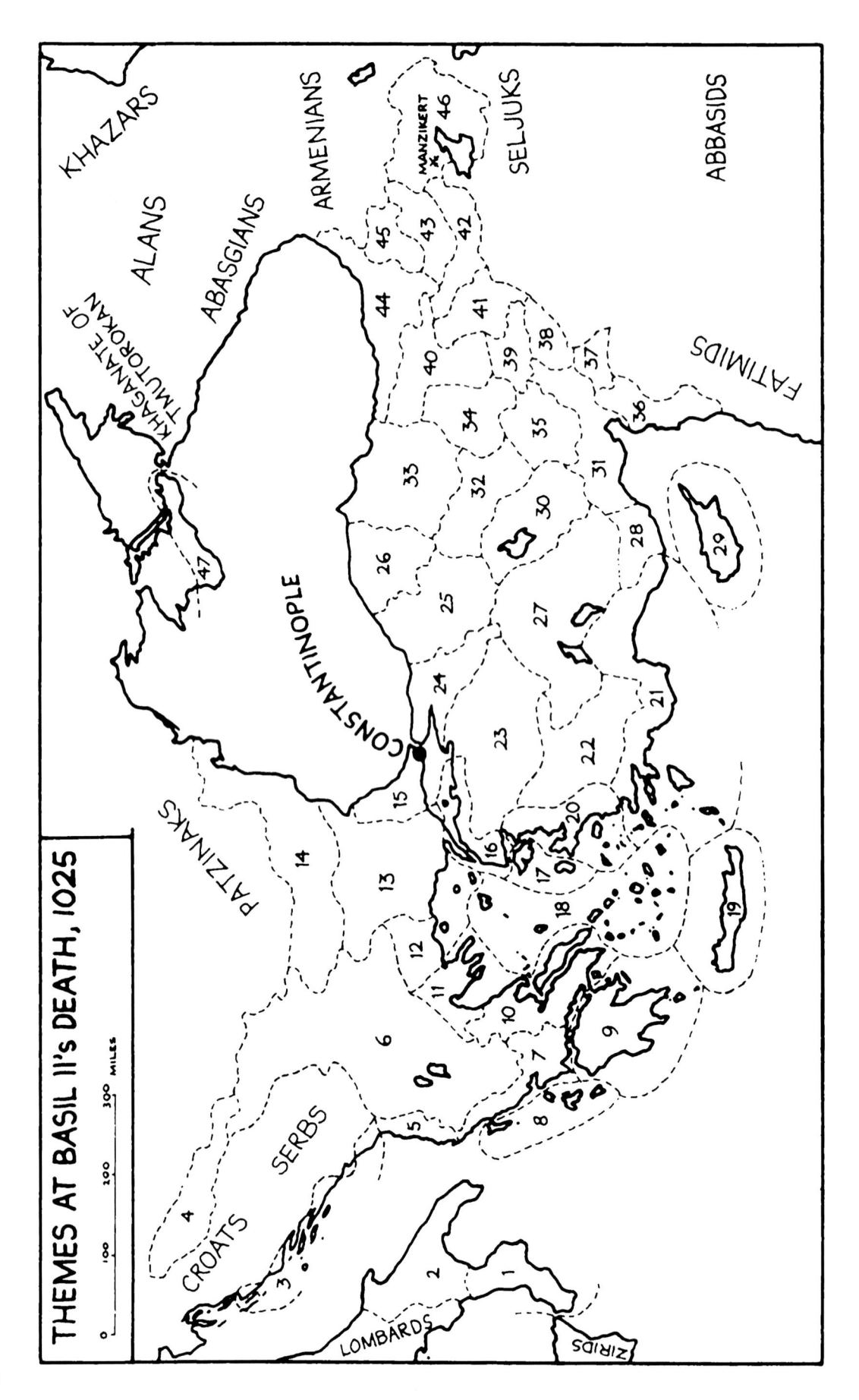

June 976 Death of Emperor Iohannes Dzimiskés from typhus (or poison). The sons of Rhomanós II Porphyrogenitus, Constantine and Basil, jointly succeed to the throne of Byzantium, but only the latter exercises actual power.

Summer 976 Várdhas Sklêrós, brother-in-law of Iohannes Dzimiskés and *Dhoméstikos* of the East, is proclaimed emperor by his troops, and defeats generals loyal to the legitimate co-emperors.

978 Várdhas Sklêrós conquers Nicaea and completes the occupation of Anatolia, approaching Constantinople.

24 May Várdhas Phokás, nephew of former Emperor Nikêphóros, defeats the usurper near Amorium, and compels him to seek refuge with the Caliph of Baghdad.

986 First Bulgarian campaign of Emperor Basil II against Comitopules, whose youngest son, Samuel, restores the late Czar Simeon's Bulgarian empire; Larissas is conquered by the Bulgarians; Basil attempts to attack Serdica by passing through the so-called 'Trajan's Door' pass, but the Imperial army is repelled.

15 August 987 Várdhas Phokás leads a revolt in Anatolia, and agrees to partition the empire with the pretender Várdhas Sklêrós.

OPPOSITE PAGE

Key to map: 1 Kalabria; 2 Langobardia; 3 Dalmatia; 4 Sirmium; 5 Dyrrachium; 6 Bulgaria; 7 Nikopolis; 8 Kephalonia; 9 Peloponnesos; 10 Hellas; 11 Thessalonika; 12 Strymon; 13 Macedonia; 14 Paristrion; 15 Thrace; 16 Abydos; 17 Chios; 18 Aegean Peleghos; 19 Krete; 20 Samos; 21 Kibyrrhaiots; 22 Thrakesion; 23 Opsikion; 24 Optimaton; 25 Bukellarion; 26 Paphlagonia; 27 Anatolikon; 28 Seleukeia; 29 Kypros; 30 Kappadocia; 31 Kilikia; 32 Charsianon; 33 Armeniakon; 34 Sebasteia; 35 Lykandos; 36 Antiocheia; 37 Teluch; 38 Poleis Parephratidiai (Euphrates Cities); 39 Melitene; 40 Koloneia; 41 Mesopotamia; 42 Taron; 43 Iberia; 44 Chaldia; 45 Theodosiopolis (Taik); 46 Vaspurakan; 47 Cherson (Gothia). In addition the Serbs and Croats, assorted Armenian and Iberian principalities, the Lombard principalities of Salerno, Capua and Benevento, and the Amirate of Aleppo all paid tribute, while Venice, Naples, Amalfi and Gaeta were still nominally Byzantine towns. (Map by Ian Heath)

LEFT

The Martyrdom of St Euphrasia – detail from an image of c. AD 1000. The man's light red garment, bearing a rhomboidal pattern in brown, is a clear example of 'soft armour' – the padded *nevrikon*. Centred in each rhomboid is a light blue dot (rivet?), silvered in the middle. The sleeves are of the removable sort, here attached with buttons at the shoulders; the cuffs are embroidered in black and gold. The sash is green, the cloak light yellow with a light blue border. The light blue trousers are chequered and embroidered with yellow flowers, and are tucked into boots which are shown as gold. The scabbard is black with yellow fittings, and the baldric is black. (*Menologion* of Basil II, folio 333 detail, Biblioteca Apostolica Vaticana, Rome; facsimile by Pio Franchi de Cavalieri, author's collection)

OPPOSITE BOTTOM PICTURE
Joshua and the Angel, in a miniature from an illuminated manuscript of c. AD 1000 that clearly shows the appearance of superior commanders of the Imperial Tághmata. Joshua (left) has a gilded ringmail *lôrikion*, well fitted to the body by means of a brown leather harness, worn over a gilded *zoupa*; his scabbard is scarlet with a gold chape. His shining helmet, of pointed outline, is shown in silver and light blue, and is fitted with a leather *peritrachelion* neck-guard. He wears a light blue tunic with white embroidery, and green *anaxyrides* with a silver netted pattern. The kneeling general wears a purple-violet *chiton* with gold dots, and gold-embroidered red trousers; his boots are painted in silver. St Michael (right) has a gilded *klivanion*; his purple-violet tunic and light blue cloak are both gold-embroidered; his green *anaxyrides* are embroidered with silver thread, and his red boots are decorated in silver. Note the light blue ribbon (*vitta*) around his head, bearing a central red stone. The scabbard and baldric are scarlet with gold fittings. (*Menologion* of Basil II, folio 3, Turin National Library; facsimile by Pio Franchi de Cavalieri, author's collection)

Spring 988 At Emperor Basil II's request, a *druzhina* of 6,000 Rus-Varangian troops are sent by Prince Vladimir of Kiev to put themselves at his disposal; they win their first victory for him near Chrysopolis.

13 April 989 Battle of Abydus; Basil's army, mostly formed from the Rus-Varangian *druzhina*, decisively defeats the usurper Várdhas Phokás, who dies of heart failure on the battlefield; end of the civil war.

Spring 991 Second Balkan campaign of Basil II.

994 Renewed invasion of Syria by the Fatimids; the Eastern Byzantine army is beaten on the Orontes river, and Aleppo is besieged.

995 *Basil surprises the enemy under the walls of Aleppo, and wins repeated victories; Raphanea and Emesa are occupied.*

997 Samuel of Bulgaria, taking advantage of the emperor's absence, enters Greece and advances as far as the Peloponnese, *but is beaten and seriously wounded by the army of the* Stratêgós Nikêphóros Ouranós.

998 The Imperial Fleet suffers a setback outside the harbour of Tyre.

999 Truce concluded between Basil II and the Fatimids.

1001–1004 *Third Balkan campaign of Basil II; Serdica, Pliska and Preslav are occupied; Imperial authority is firmly re-established in northern Greece; Byzantine armies defeat the Bulgarians on the Vardar river and conquer Vodena, Vidin and Skoplj.*

1005 *Dyrrachium recaptured.*

July–September 1014 *The Bulgarian army, trapped at Kleidon's Gorge, is surrounded and destroyed; 14,000 prisoners are blinded, and sent back to Czar Samuel in groups of 100 each led by a man blind in only one eye; two days after being confronted by this spectacle, the Bulgarian czar dies.*

1017 A strong army is sent to Italy under the *Katépano* Basil Boiannes, in response to a revolt organized by Melos of Bari.

February 1018 Basil II enters Ochrida, Bulgaria, in triumph; end of the first Bulgarian Empire. After four centuries of Slav-Bulgarian domination, the whole Balkans are once again under Eastern Roman rule.

1020 Basil Boioannes, supported by Norman mercenaries, inflicts a heavy defeat on the Lombard rebels at Cannae. Civil war in Armenia leads to Imperial intervention, and annexation of the whole country to Byzantine territory.

1025 *Basil sends a strong army with a fleet to pacify Italy and to regain Sicily; the Islamic Zirid fleet is destroyed by a storm before having the chance to confront the Byzantines.*

15 December 1025 Death of Emperor Basil II Porphyrogenitus; he is succeeded by Constantine VIII.

THE REGIMENTS – FORMATION & ORGANIZATION

THE *THÉMATA*

The Byzantine army of this period was the result of a development that had started in the 7th century. The then Emperor Heraclius (r.610–641) had begun to divide the Imperial territories in Anatolia into military provinces or *Thémata*, which corresponded with the provincial army corps from which the Thémata took their names: e.g., *Anatolikón, Opsíkion, Optímaton*, etc.

The Massacre of the Innocents, in an image of *c.* AD 1,000. The most interesting figure in this New Testament scene is the young royal guard (centre). His tunic is light green, embroidered with small circlets and squared spaces, and with heavy embroidery in gold around the neck and wrists and on the shoulders. The surface of the shield is light blue with red decorations and gold fittings. The model for this guardsman might have been an Imperial *Eskoubitor* of the Tághmata, since that regiment was linked to the 'Greens' faction of the Circus (Hippodrome) in Constantinople. (*Menologion* of Basil II, folio 281, Biblioteca Apostolica Vaticana, Rome; facsimile by Pio Franchi de Cavalieri, author's collection)

With the passage of time the system was extended, since it allowed an easier defence of the Eastern Byzantine borders from the repeated Muslim incursions. This system of standing provincial army corps also spread to the empire's Western fronts, and by the end of the 9th century this kind of subdivision appears to have been widely consolidated. By the death of Basil II in 1025 the whole Imperial territory apart from the region surrounding Constantinople itself was divided into 47 Thémata. Each Théma was subject to a military governor or *stratêgós*, who was also the military commander of the provincial army (*stratós*) that was stationed there. In some widespread border regions the military command was given separately to a *dhoux*, who led the army corps stationed in those places. In some Thémata a civil officer, the *protonotarios* – assisted by a *praitor* (also called a *dikasthes* or *krites*), and by a *sakellários* or *kartoularios* – supervised the juridical and financial administration.

The provincial army corps were composed partly of professional soldiers (*stratiotes*), and

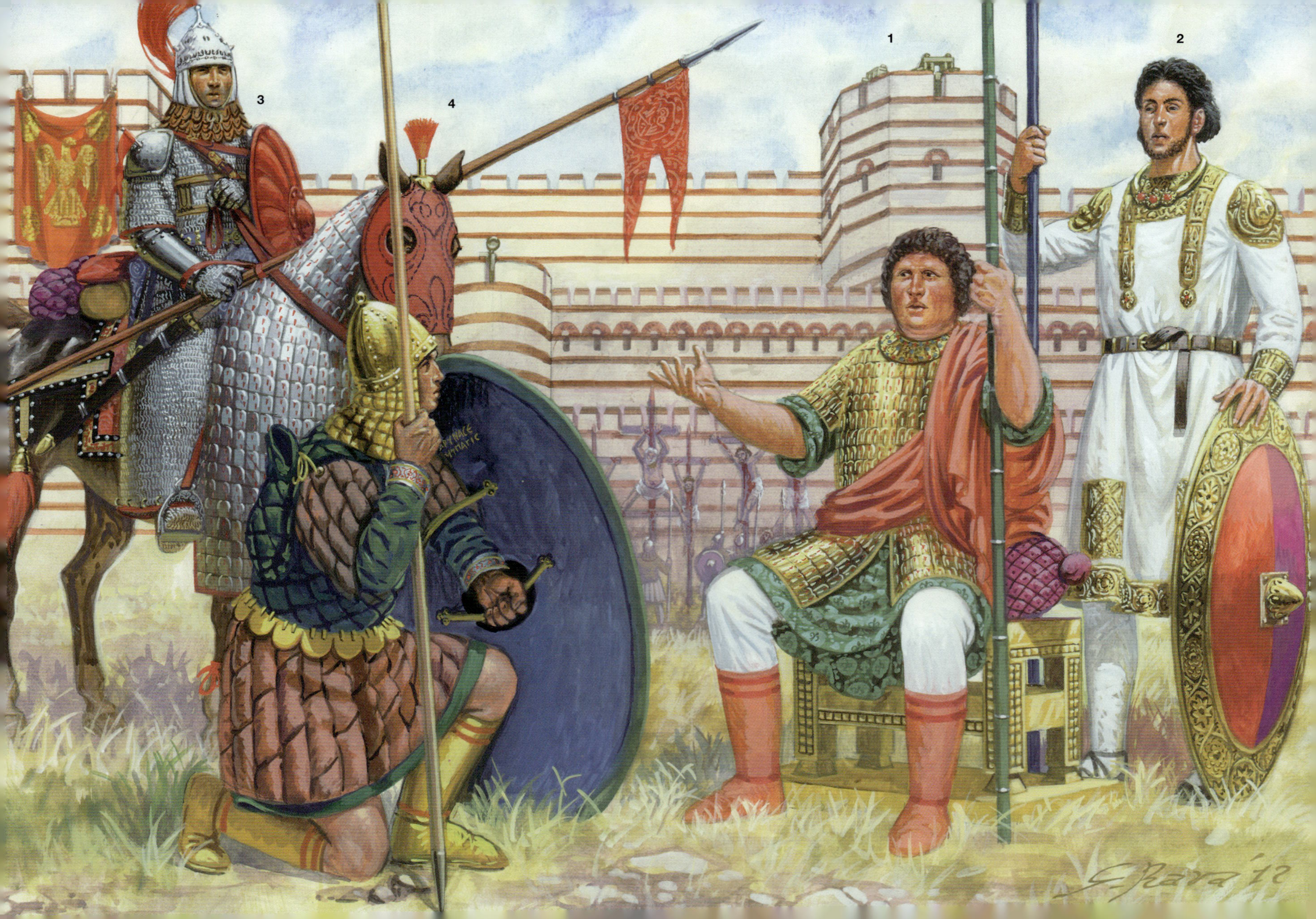
3
4
1
2

partly of local farmer-soldiers, who in exchange for periodic military service to the state were granted small land holdings. Both the land and the military obligation passed by inheritance to their sons, continued title to the former depending upon continued fulfillment of the latter. (Both professional and part-time soldiers were paid, however.) These Thematic armies constituted the military frontier forces of the Byzantine Empire, and were the true advocates of the 'age of reconquest'. For much of this period the Eastern Thémata were predominant, and the elite *Théma Anatólikon* excelled above all. The soldiers of the Imperial *Tághmata* were often recruited among the Thematics.

THE *TÁGHMATA*

The territory of Constantinople and its surrounding regions was not organized as a Théma. The defence of the capital was guaranteed by the presence there, or within a practical distance, of a central field army. (This was stationed in the Thracian district called Tafla or Talaya in Islamic sources, in Macedonia in the west, and in Bithynia in the east.) These regiments formed the elite Imperial *Tághmata*; the cavalry joined the emperor on his military expeditions or manoeuvred to protect the capital when it came under threat, together with the infantry which normally formed the garrison of the city. These were the regiments that, at the moment of the appointment of a new *Avtokrator* or *Vasiléfs* (emperor), expressed the consensus of the whole army by raising the newly elected emperor on their shields. Collectively, this army was the spearhead during the Byzantine counter-offensives against the Arabs and Bulgarians in the 9th–10th centuries.

Set of Eastern Roman *lamellae* found near Strumica, Macedonia. This exceptional find is probably what it is left of the armour of a heavy archer *kataphraktos*. The long *lamellae* are each punched with two holes at the top corners and two centred on each side, for fastening. (Photo courtesy Prof Vane Sekulov, Strumica Museum)

A: OFFICERS AND SOLDIERS PREPARING FOR THE BULGARIAN SIEGE, AUGUST 913

1: *Katépanos* of *Vasilikoi Anthropoi*
This senior officer of the 'Imperials' of the Guard is wearing a gilded *thorax folidotos* (scale corselet), covered by a crimson *sagion* (military cloak). Note the high pinkish-red boots (*kampotouvia*). The colours here are restored from the original pigments of a Joshua plaque now in the Metropolitan Museum of Art.

2: *Primikérios Kandidatos* of VIII *Skhóla*
The *kandidatos*, reconstructed from folio 215v of the *Commentaries of St Gregorius Nazianzenus* now in the Bibliothéque Nationale in Paris, wears the costly representative parade uniform (*allaxima*) of his unit. The white *kandidatikion* is furnished with a richly decorated collar (*maniakion*), and decorated with gold *klavoi* and *orbiculi*. The gold *epikarpia* on his wrists are copied from the Thessaloniki specimen. He is armed with a spear of Frankish type, with a 'winged' head (obscured here. The colours of his richly decorated *skoutarion* could be the *semeion* of either V or VIII *Skhóla*.

3: *Kavallarios Kataphraktos* of III *Skhóla*
This heavy cavalryman is reconstructed according to a description of the *kataphraktoi* in Leo VI's *Tactiká* and *Sylloge Tacticorum*. His neck armour is an old-style *peritrachelion*. Note his two swords (the baldric indicates the second, slung from his right shoulder) and mace. Leo's *Tactiká* (VI, 31) mentions the horse armour: 'They armoured the horses with side and front pieces, i.e. the horses' flanks, heads and necks, with plates or iron mail, or… with other material'. According to the *Sylloge*, the heads were protected by *prometopidiai* (brow-pieces) and the necks and breasts by small iron scales or plates.

4: *Skoutatos* of *Noúmeroi*
A typical heavy infantryman of the period, serving in one of the two regiments of the Constantinople garrison. The colours have been reconstructed from the Metropolitan Museum plaque. His coloured *epanoklivanian/epilorikion*, worn over his *klivanion*, as well as his padded *nevrikon*, were probably in the distinctive colours of his company (*vándon*).

Background: In front of the walls of Constantinople, light cavalrymen of the *Víghla* are executing heretic Bogomils.

St Theodore Stratilates was the patron saint of the *Athanatoi* Tághma, whose appearance may have been the model for this representation of the saint. (This image was probably carried on the regiment's main flag.) The little *omega* on the shield, recalling God's words 'I am the Alpha and the Omega', reflects the conception of the 'eternal' life – another possible association with a regiment named 'the Immortals'. The sleeved *roukhon* is in purple, decorated with small gold-embroidered circlets and quadrates on its surface and with gold-thread cuffs and borders. (*Menologion* of Basil II, folio 383, Biblioteca Apostolica Vaticana, Rome; facsimile by Pio Franchi de Cavalieri, author's collection)

The Tághmata was composed of professional soldiers – paid, long-service mercenaries – who were recruited both inside and outside the territory of the empire. Detachments of the Tághmata were also stationed in the provinces, where they operated under the direction of their own officers responding to the local *dhoukes* or *stratêgói*. Indeed, in the period of the great Arab attacks by the Emir Saif ad-Dawla, the central army was constantly present in the border regions, and the unified command of the whole army under the *Dhoméstikos* of the *Skhólai* assured the co-ordination of defensive and offensive operations by Thematic and Taghmatic troops. The 11th century was characterized by an increase in the Taghmatic units directly created by the central power, and a corresponding decrease in the numbers of Thematic contingents.

The soldiers composing the Tághmata were under the administrative supervision of the *Logothétês tou Stratiotikoù*, the Imperial minister responsible for military affairs, whose office (*logothésion*) compiled and updated the *katalogoi* (lists) of the enlisted troops, and provided their salaries (*rogai*).

The Tághmata of this period comprised five elite regiments: the *Skhólai*, *Exkoúvitoi* or *Exkoubitores*, *Ikanátoi*, *Vighla* or *Arithmós*, and – from AD 970 – the *Athanatoi*. In a wider sense, the denomination Tághmata also embraced parts of the Imperial Guard, the infantry regiments which defended Constantinople – the *Noúmeroi* and *Teichistai* – and also the units of the *Vasilikoploimon*, the Imperial war fleet stationed at Constantinople.

THE *SKHÓLAI*

The Tághma of *Skhólai* was the most important and certainly the oldest in the whole army, since it originated in the *Scholae Palatinae* units created by Constantine the Great at the beginning of the 4th century. The 5th-century *Notitia Dignitatum* lists seven *Scholae* for the Eastern Empire. In time their role of palace guardsmen reduced their campaign effectiveness, but during the reign of Constantine V in the mid-8th century they were reorganized to restore their military value. They became an efficient cavalry field force, the spearhead of the renewed offensive capability of the empire in the 9th and 10th centuries.

According to a treatise by Nikêphóros Ouranós, probably written for the emperor on the occasion of Basil II's second campaign against the Bulgarians, during the 10th century the *Skhólai* were organized in 30 *vánda*.[1] Since the 6th century the *vándon* had been the classic tactical unit, and in the 10th century the term might refer to a strength of either 300–400 men

---

1 Note that depending upon the convention adopted for transliteration from Greek, the Roman letters 'v' and 'b' may be interchangeable. Thus, *vándon* or *bandon*, *klivanion* or *klibanion*, etc. We have not imposed absolute consistency in this text, but generally use 'v'.

(according to the *Taktika* of Leo VI the Wise, *c*. 903, and the roughly contemporaneous *Sylloge Tacticorum*), or of only 50 (according to the *Praecepta Militaria* of the Emperor Nikêphóros Phokás). Indeed, with reference to the palace units the figure of 50 men per *vándon* is more probable, giving a total of 1,500 *Skholárioi*. In any case, we should consider such numbers as purely indicative. New levies of Taghmatic soldiers were made on the occasion of large military expeditions or offensive operations: e.g. 1,037 *Skholárioi* from Thrace and Macedonia (about 20 *vánda*) participated in the 911 expedition against Crete. For his campaigns against the Arabs, Nikêphóros Phokás increased the number of the Taghmatic *vánda* by strengthening the extra-heavy cavalry termed at that time *klivanophoroi* (horsemen wearing the heavy armour called the *klivanion*). In the whole Tághmata there were probably three units of *klivanophoroi*, of strengths varying between 384 and 504 men.

Officer ranks and appointments

The commander of the *Skhólai* had the title of *Dhoméstikos*, inherited from a Late Roman subordinate of the *Magister Officiorum*, the first among the civilian functionaries of the empire. However, in 767 Constantine V used this title for a completely new rank to command the newly reorganized *Skhólai*. In the period considered here the *Dhoméstikos* of the *Skhólai* was the most senior officer of the whole Imperial Tághmata, supreme commander of the army in the absence of the emperor, and *Stratêgós* of the *Théma Anatolikon*. In the usual Byzantine fashion, the officer holding this military appointment simultaneously held parallel Imperial court titles and dignities – those of *Anthypatos* and *Patríkios*, usually associated in his case with the rank or status of *Protospathários*, 'first among the sword-bearers' (our sources are the 9th/ 10th-century *Kletorologion* of Phylotheus, the *Taktikón* Benesevic, and the *Taktikón* held in the Escorial Palace library). From the reign of Rhomanós I (r.920–944) the appointment was duplicated, with *Dhoméstikoi* for the Western and Eastern *Skhólai*; however, only the Eastern officer was called *Megas Dhoméstikos* ('Great...'), and received all the titles and dignities mentioned.[2]

Directly subordinate to the *Dhoméstikos* was the *Topotêrêtes* ('vice' or 'substitute'), who sometimes received the Imperial dignity of *Spathárokandidatos* (according to the *Kletorologion* of Phylotheus, AD 899). His substitute role, especially in the 10th–11th centuries, is indicated in the treatise *De velitatione bellica* attributed to Nikêphóros Phokás, in which the *Topotêrêtes* is listed as the operational commander of the possible Taghmatic regiment present in the theatre of war. Again, the *Topotêrêtes* led the 869 *Skholárioi* stationed in Thrace and Macedonia who participated in the expedition against Crete in the year 969. We should remember that in this period the supreme army command role of the *Megas Dhoméstikos* made it necessary for him to delegate a part of his operational command function to an immediate subordinate. By at latest

One of a pair of 9th–11th century spurs of gilded iron; the detailed decoration of this remarkable find leaves no doubt about their Byzantine origin, although they were found in a Bulgarian hoard at Pimensko. (Photo courtesy Prof Valeri Yotov)

---

2 For a note on parallel military/ court titles held by senior figures in the Imperial service, see below under 'The Imperial Guard – The *Vasilikoi Anthropoi*'.

Iohannes, a *Proximos* with the court rank of *Protospathários*, who served under the *Dhoux* Theodorakan in the *Théma* of Armenia; for reconstruction, see Plate G1. Note his gilded *klivanion* with double rivets. The way in which the *klivanion* was fastened is still difficult to understand, but in this miniature portrait of an Armenian Imperial officer of c. 1007, we note that his corselet is fastened on the shoulders. (Armenian Adrianople Gospel, Mechitarist Library, Venice; author's photo from original)

the early 970s, when the Escorial *Taktikón* was written, there were two *Topotêrêtai*.

Third in rank among the senior *offikialoi* of the *Skhólai* was the *Kartoularios*, with the Imperial dignity of *Spathários*, who was responsible for the whole administration of the regiment, e.g. the enlistment and payment of the troops. His duties differed from those of analogous Thematic officers in that he also had an important operational role as commander of half the regiment under the *Topotêrêtes* when the *Skhólai* went to war without the *Dhoméstikos*.

The individual *vánda* were commanded by *kómites*, who enjoyed the dignity of Imperial *Spatharioi*. Under them were officers called – confusingly – *dhoméstikoi*, second in rank and having the Imperial status of *Stratores* ('shield-bearers'). In a 50-man unit they commanded a *dekarchia* or line of ten troopers. These officers were the direct descendants of the *domestici protectores* of the Late Roman Empire. The *Notitia Dignitatum* and other sources of the Late Empire make a distinction between *domestici equitum* and *domestici peditum*, and the fact that the *Liber de Ceremoniis* still mentions *dhoméstikoi peditou* and *skholárioi peditou* confirms the existence, at the beginning of the 10th century, of the infantry *vándon* as a sub-unit among the *Skhólai*.

The rank of *Dhoméstikos* was also held by the officer appointed as *Proximos*, and the importance of this appointment had increased in exactly the period under consideration. From an officer with the function of maintaining the contacts between the junior and senior ranks of a *Tághma*, he had been assigned to the entourage of the emperor both at court and during military campaigns, to manage special missions for the emperor and to act as liaison officer between him and the Taghmatic regiments. The *Anonymus de re militari* informs us that in camp his tent was pitched beside those of the *Kómês ton Voukinon* (the commanders of the trumpeters), so as to form a military staff ready to transmit the operational commands of the emperor or the *Dhoméstikos*. A letter of Rhomanós I informs us of a diplomatic mission performed in Armenia by the *Spathárokandidatos* and *Proximos* Konstantinos.

Next in rank were the junior officer standard-bearers of the regiment: the *protiktores*, the *eutychophoroi*, the *skeptrophoroi* (with status inferior to that of *Stratores*), and under them the *axiomatikoi* and the *mandátores*.

The *protiktores* were descended directly from the bodyguards of the Late Roman *Dominus*, the *Custodes Divini Lateris*. Incorporated in the *Domestici* and then in the *Scholae* during the 6th–7th centuries, they now had the role of

Bronze buckle, 10th–11th century, from recent excavations in the Sacred Palace of Constantinople. This kind of buckle was widely used by military men for belts, and also for the side fastening of *klivania*. (Istanbul Archaeological Museum; author's photo)

10th–11th century bronze fastening – perhaps a strap junction from horse harness? – excavated in the Sacred Palace of Constantinople. (Istanbul Archaeological Museum, author's photo)

bearers of the *skevi* – a generic word that in the *Liber de Ceremoniis Aulae Byzantinae* of Constantine Porphyrogenitus denotes the Imperial emblems. In this case, however, it could be synonymous with the golden shafts also called *trophea*, mounting representations of arms and armour. In this period *protiktores*, *dhoméstikoi* and *kómites* were still appointed to their ranks directly by the emperor himself, in a ceremony that took place in the presence of the *Dhoméstikos ton Skholón*, during which the officer was handed a document termed the *provatoreia* or *chartion*, attesting to his investiture.

The *eutychophoroi* bore the seven *eutykia* or *ptykia*, the standards with the image of Fortuna and of the Winged Victory inherited from the triumphal symbols of ancient Rome. The *skeptrophoroi*, with the status of *Kandidatoi*, bore the 15 *Romaikà sképtra*, i.e. the Roman consular sceptres; some of them, topped with a cross or an eagle and covered with purple cloth, were called *Víla*. It is probable that these three categories of standard-bearers were attached to the staff of each *kómês*.

The *axiomatikoi*, according to Haldon, were the simple junior officers of the *Skhólai* – the equivalent of the old *ducenarii* and *centenarii* of the *Scholae Palatinae*. Following the reforms of Constantine V these had seen their importance reduced, but kept their

(continued on page 20)

The Slaying of the Holy Fathers on Sinai. This detail from a miniature of the turn of the 10th/11th centuries shows images of Imperial infantrymen, probably copied from the Constantinople garrison regiments. The headwear is the typical turban or *phakeolion*, those of alternate figures here being coloured violet-red and dark green. The military tunics are (from left to right) green, red, and white stripes; light blue with gold circlets; and dark red chequered with silver circlets, opening on the right and white-lined. All the embroidery round the cuffs is in gold thread. The trousers are (from left to right) scarlet embroidered in light yellow; violet-red with green-yellow lines and white dots; and green with gold embroidery. The low boots are white and silver. Note also the command sash of the officer in the foreground, probably the *pektorarin* or *loros* of the sources. The swords are in silver; the scabbards are black with white fittings, and dark red with yellow fittings. The small *cheiroskoutaria* shields are in red with a silver rim, and light blue with white dots and gold rim. (*Menologion* of Basil II, folio 316, Biblioteca Apostolica Vaticana, Rome; facsimile by Pio Franchi de Cavalieri, author's collection)

B: PALACE CEREMONY, 31 MAY 946

1: Guardsman of the Imperial *Manglavion*

Posed on steps in the Imperial palace, this figure is again reconstructed from the St Gregorius Nazianzenus manuscript, with the red *skaramangion* and trousers of the Imperial *Maghlavítai* which echoed the dress of the old Roman *lictores*. The long-shafted mace, and the golden whip in his belt, are symbolic of the duties and prerogatives of this unit; their 'police' role was not simply ceremonial, and they were empowered to inflict punishments up to and including death. Note his sword, furnished with a sleeve-like extension of the hilt down the blade below the crossguard.

2: *Strator* of the *Vasilikoi Anthropoi*

This Imperial squire, originally from a far-flung territory, is dressed in a long and splendid *skaramangion* ornamented with white lions (*levkoleontai*). The *stratorikion* (staff) is a symbol of his rank, probably derived from the officer's staves of the Late Roman Empire.

3: Macedonian Guardsman of the *Méghalhe Etaireía*

The most loyal element of the Porphyrogenitus dynasty's 1,000-strong *Vasilikê Etaireía* were distinguished on special occasions by their precious silvered swords and gilded shields, and wore sashes of cloth of gold or silver. Note his highly decorated felt and leather armour, and, carried behind his shield, his single-bladed axe. The source for this Guardsman is the representation of St Merkourios from the Church of St George at Belisarama, Cappadocia.

4: Khazar warrior of the *Mhese Etaireía*

'At the bottom, on the last steps, stood the soldiers of the Middle and Great *Etaireía* – *Pharganoi* and Khazars – all of them wearing swords and holding shields' (*De Cer.*, II, 576). This Khazar Guardsman is based on an archaeological reconstruction by Dr M.V. Gorelik, but part of his military equipment is from Byzantine arsenals. The origin of the *skaramangion* in the Euro-Asiatic horseman's kaftan is noticeable here. Note the band around his brow – this bears an inscription with the name of his unit commander. He parades with a drawn sabre; note that a bowcase slung from the left side of his belt would balance the quiver.

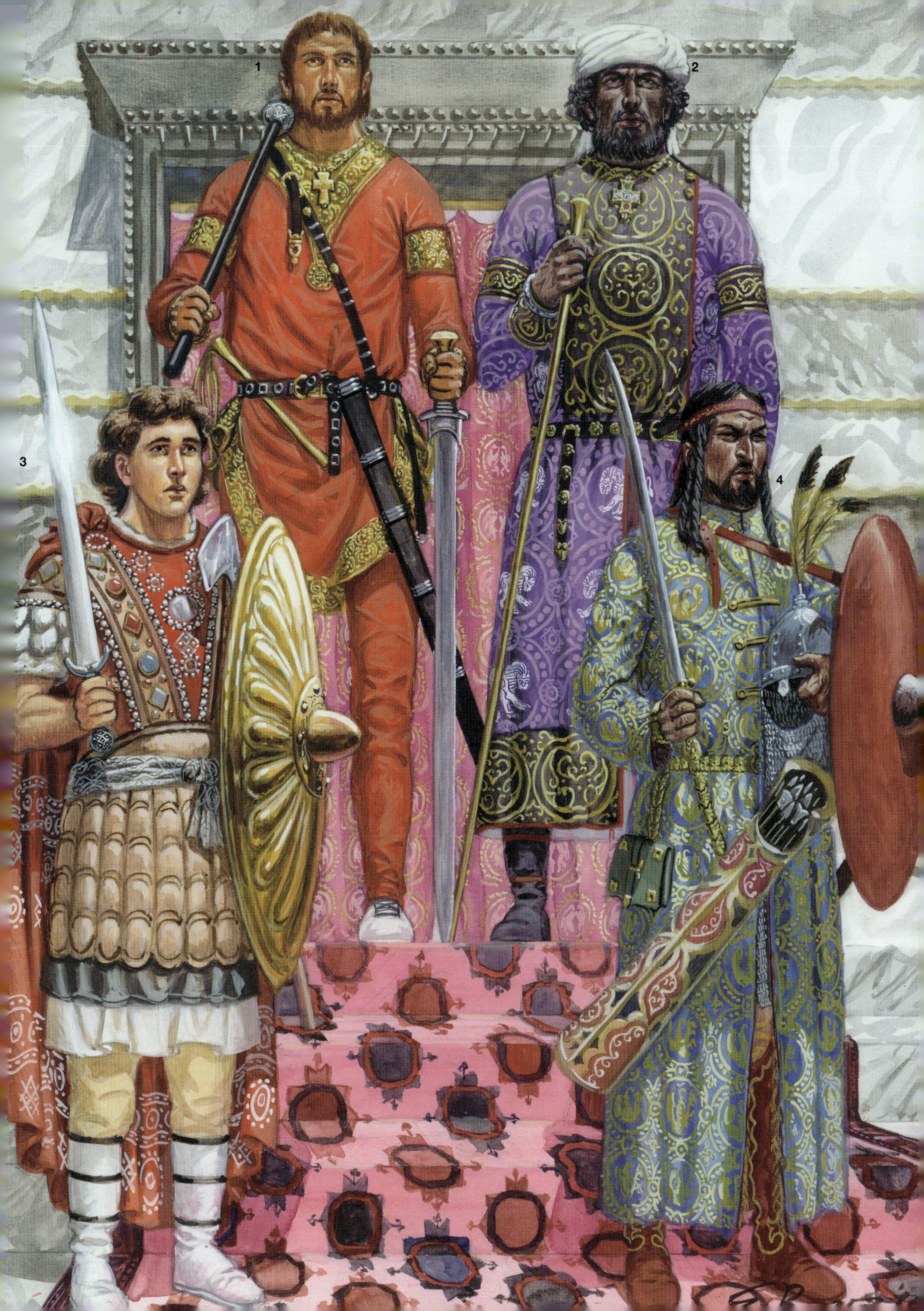
1
2
3
4

official function of escorting during official ceremonies those who were invested with a dignity or *axioma*.

Serving directly under the *Proximos* were the *mandátores* ('messengers'), who provided liaison between different units or inside a single *vándon*. According to the *Taktiká* of Leo (XI, 20), each officer with the rank of *kómês* or above should have a *mandátor* at the disposition of his immediate superior officer, for the prompt transmission of his orders.

Last in the hierarchy were the simple *Skholárioi Tághmatikoi*, the soldiers of the regiment.

THE *ESKOUBITORES*

This second regiment of the Tághmata was created in the second half of the 5th century by the Emperor Leo I the Thracian, with the purpose of creating a body of 300 fighting guardsmen more effective than the *Scholae Palatinae*. However, this unit too had lost much of its effectiveness before the 8th-century reforms of Constantine V put it alongside the *Skhólai* in the new field army.

In the year 949 the *Liber de Ceremoniis* mentions 700 *Eskoubitores* with all their officers. However, this reference is only to the contingents in the capital, called '*Peratics*' (from the name of the quarter of Sykai-Peran, on the opposite side of the Golden Horn waterway). Considering that sections of this Tághma were also located in Thrace and Macedonia, we might consider a total strength of 900 *Eskoubitores* reasonable. This would accord with the reference in the *Vita Ioannici* that mentions 18 *vánda* of *Eskoubitores* for the period immediately following the reforms of Constantine V.

Officer ranks and appointments

In 765 the command of this regiment was given to a *Dhoméstikos*, replacing the old *Comes Excubitorum* of the Late Roman period. Sources of the late 9th century and the *Kletorologion* of Phyloteus (pp. 111–113) give to him the status of *Protospathários* and the Imperial dignities of *Patríkios* and *Anthypatos*. The 10th-century *Taktikón* of the Escorial even mentions three *dhoméstikoi*: one for the Eastern *Exkoubitorei*, one for the Western, and a third, of slightly lower status, for the unit stationed inside the walls of Constantinople. However, this triplication must have been only temporary, because the 11th-century sources mention only a single commander of the *Eskoubitores*.

Within this Tághma too a *Topotêrêtes* – in our period, with the Imperial status of *Spathárokandidatos* – commanded the whole unit when the *Dhoméstikos* was absent, his duties being similar to those of his counterpart in the *Skhólai*. The triplication of the command of the *Eskoubitores* during the 10th century may explain why both the *Liber de Ceremoniis* and the Escorial *Taktikón* mention or suggest the existence of more than one *Topotêrêtai*.

Next came the *Kartoularios*, with the Imperial dignity of *Spathários*, whose functions and duties were substantially identical in all the regiments of the Tághmata. The individual *vánda* within the *Eskoubitores* were commanded by *skribones*, with the Imperial status of *Stratóres*, who corresponded to the *kómites* of the *Skhólai*. (These senior officers of the Tághma should not be confused with the *deputatoi skribones*, who, according to the *Taktiká* of Leo VI, were attached to each Taghmatic and Thematic unit with the duty of recovering wounded men on the battlefield.)

After the *Protomandátor* – an officer similar in functions to the *Proximos* of *Skhólai* – the junior officers of the *Eskoubitores* were standard-bearers with the ranks of *drakonarioi*, *skeuophoroi*, *signophoroi* and *sinatores*.

Warrior of the *Méghali Etaireía* (Great *Etaireía*) of the Imperial Guard, recruited from Macedonians and other Christian subjects from the heartlands of the empire; and (right) a 'marine' soldier of the *Vasilikodhrómonion*. Their corselets are silvered and gilded, with white *kremasmata* on the lower border; the boots are in silver and gold with white dots. Under their armour they wear green and red tunics, one with gold embroidery. The artist has represented both (left) a gilded bronze shield, and the leather shield (*dorka*) mentioned in *De Ceremoniis* for the naval troops. The spears are painted in brown and green. (*Menologion* of Basil II, folio 62 detail, Biblioteca Apostolica Vaticana, Rome; facsimile by Pio Franchi de Cavalieri, author's collection)

Apart from their main role as standard-bearers, the *drakonarioi* had duties within the *vánda* corresponding to those of the junior *dhoméstikoi* of the *Skhólai*, as assumed after the reforms of Constantine V. They bore – with fierce pride – the 12 *drakontia*, which in peacetime were kept in the Church of the Lord inside the Sacred Palace. (The *draco*, which in Late Roman times had become the common standard of the *legiones* and *vexillationes*, was now mainly limited to the elite Guard regiments.)

True flags were carried by 18 officers generically called *skeuophoroi*; this was the number of standard-poles kept in the Church of the Lord, corresponding with the presumptive number of *vánda* of *Eskoubitores*. Other standard-bearers, the *signophoroi*, carried the *signa* or *semeia*; these were either Imperial banners of purple cloth embroidered in gold with images of the emperor, or shafts bearing such images in gilded wood.

With the reforms of Constantine V the *sinatores* had lost their original role of senior officers of the regiment, immediately subordinate to the old *Comes Excubitorum* and his *Domesticus* in the Late Roman period; now they were simply junior officers bearing *skevi* standards and flags.

ABOVE
11th-century fresco showing an Imperial Guard cavalryman performing displays or games in the Hippodrome of Constantinople. (St Sophia Museum, Kiev; author's photo, courtesy of the Museum)

The ranks of the *Eskoubitores* included the *legatarioi mandátores*, directly subordinate to the *Protomandátor*. In addition to their military functions as messengers, they also retained the city police duties typical of their Late Roman forerunners.

THE '*VIGLA*' OR '*ARITHMÓS*'

In AD 786 the Empress Irene ordered the cavalry troopers of the *Théma Thrakésion* (the *Vexillationes Arithmói*), under their commanders (*kómites* and *dhroungárioi*), to rush to Constantinople to strengthen her control over the capital. One of these regiments – perhaps the *Comites Arcadiaci* – was transformed into a new Tághma loyal only to her, the *Víghla* or *Vigilia*. During the reign of Nikêphóros I (r.802–811) the *Víghla* became, for all intents and purposes, an operational Taghmatic regiment.

It is clear from the *Liber de Ceremoniis* that in the 10th century this Tághma mainly had the duty of ensuring the emperor's security and protecting the Sacred Palace, as well as guarding the Constantinople Hippodrome. The name itself, from the Latin *vigilia*, is synonymous by extension with watchmen, guards or patrols, referring to its duties within the walls of the capital. We have no reference to its numerical strength, but it probably had a similar structure to the other Tághmata, being divided into *vánda* each of 50 men.

RIGHT
Detail of the fresco showing a Guard cavalryman; for these occasions – recalling the 'cavalry sports' of the old Roman Empire – the shield (*skoutarion*) appears to be richly decorated, with real or simulated gemstones. (St Sophia Museum, Kiev; author's photo, courtesy of the Museum)

Officer ranks and appointments

The commander still had the title of *Dhroungários*, the Imperial dignity of *Anthypatos* and *Patríkios*, and the status of *Protospathários*. At the beginning of the 11th century his military functions became subordinate to those he fulfilled as the judicial official in charge of palace security on the Tribunal of the *Maghnávra*. Under him, a *Topotêrêtes Spathárokandidatos* and a *Kartoularios* performed inside the *Víghla* the duties of their counterparts in the other *Tághmata*.

More interesting was the transformation that we see in the figure of the *Akolouthos* ('follower'), who originally fulfilled the same administrative functions as the *Proximos* and *Protomandátor*, and was responsible for the foreigners who enlisted in the *Tághma*. When the *Dhroungários* became in practice a judicial officer, the *Akolouthos* became an independent senior officer, and commander of the famous Varangian Guard (see below).

The individual *vánda* were commanded by *kómites*, seconded by their immediate subordinates the *kentarkai* (from the Late Roman *centenarii*, descended in turn from the old Roman *centuriones*). The *Víghla* had its own standard-bearers. The *bandophoroi* carried true military flags or *vánda*, which were of rectangular or squared shape terminating in smaller pointed streamers (*flamoulae*); this was, since the 6th century, the most typical standard of the Eastern Roman army. The *lavouresioi* were assigned to carry the five *lavara*, the most ancient Romano-Christian standards, which in peacetime were kept inside the Great Palace. These were squared cloths hanging vertically from a wooden pole with a cross-shaft, and were embroidered with the cross or the Christian 'Chi-Rho' monogram. The *semeiophoroi* carried the *semeia*, the Imperial bust images embroidered in gold on purple cloth. The *doukiniatores* – derived from the Late Roman rank of *ducenarius* – were standard-bearers similar in rank to the *sinatores* of the *Eskoubitores*; they carried the *kampiduktoria*, probably cross-shaped standards descended from the *insignia* staves borne by the Late Roman *campiductores* at the head of their soldiers.

The *Víghla*, too, had their *mandátores*, and beside them the *legatarioi* and *diatrekontes*, who fulfilled the duties, respectively, of city police and messengers of the *Dhroungários*. However, the *diatrekontes* also provided, together with the *skoutarioi*, the true fighters of the unit. The former performed the function of troopers (*kursores*); the latter, heavily armoured, formed the heavy section of the *Tághma* (the *defensores*).

When inside the city, in consequence of the unit's responsibility for guarding the Hippodrome, it also provided the *thuroroi* or door guards for that building, who served directly under the authority of the *Dhroungários*.

THE *IKANÁTOI*

Created in 809 by the *Vasiléfs* Nikêphóros I as a personal bodyguard for his son Stavrakios, this Tághma was drawn from the sons of the highest aristocracy of the empire. (The word *ikanoi* corresponded to the Latin *idonei*, and signified warriors who were of perfect age, height and

Sts Gregory of Nazianzius and Theodosius, in a miniature of c. AD 880. The Imperial *Spathárioi* or *Protospathárioi*, visible here, were equipped with a *spathion chrysokanon*, i.e. a sword with a golden hilt, as described in *De Ceremoniis* (II, 574–575, 640) and the *Kletorologion* of Philotheos (91, 127) as a distinction of the court rank of these Imperial Guardsmen. (Cod. Par. Gr. 510, folio 239r; ex Kolias)

physical strength.) The unit seems to have been structured on the model of the *Víghla*. At the beginning it was probably conceived as a unit for the training of cadet officers, but by the reign of Michael II (r.820–829) it was already an elite fighting Tághma.

According to the *Liber de Ceremoniis*, in the year 949 the *Ikanátoi* in the capital numbered 456 men, i.e. nine *vánda* of 50 enlisted men each, to which should be added the provincial squadrons of the Tághma.

The officer ranks were largely identical to those of the *Víghla*, but with some differences: the commander was not a *Dhroungários* but a *Dhoméstikos*, *Anthýpatos* and Imperial *Patríkios*, with the dignity of *Protospathários*. Instead of the *Akolouthos* we find a *Protomandátor*. Apart from that, this regiment was also officered by a *Topotêrêtes Spathárokandidatos*, a *Kartoularios*, *kómites* and *kentarchai*. The standard-bearers were termed *bandophoroi*, *doukiniatores* and *semeiophoroi*. Here again we find the *mandátores*, serving directly under the *Protomandátor*.

THE *ATHANATOI*

In AD 970 the host of Svyátoslav, Prince of Kiev – composed of Russo-Varangians and reinforced by Bulgaro-Pecheneg cavalry – sacked the city of Philippopolis and then marched directly towards the heart of the empire, Constantinople. The *Vasiléfs* Iohannes Dzimiskés, preparing for the confrontation that would see him victorious against this powerful enemy, decided to strengthen the Imperial elite troops by creating a new Tághma, to which he gave the ostentatious name of *Athanatoi*, the 'Immortals'. This echoed that of the famous royal bodyguard of the Persian Achemenids, so called because their losses suffered on the battlefield were immediately replaced so that the number in the ranks would not change. Leo the Diacon, a Greek historian of the 10th century, describes the impressive spectacle of the *Athanatoi* marching towards the enemy, shining in their gold and silver armour (Leo Diac., VIII, 4).

This Taghmatic regiment is still mentioned in the *Anonymus de re militari* at the end of the 10th century. The Escorial *Taktikón* mentions a *Dhoméstikos* of *Athanatoi*, under whom we find a *Topotêrêtes*. Otherwise the regiment was probably structured on the model of the other Tághmata.

THE *NOÚMEROI* AND *TEICHISTAI*

The *demoi* or quarters into which the capital city was divided corresponded with the old factions among the crowd of the Circus, which identified themselves by the four traditional colours of blue, green, white and red. These districts contributed to the defence of the city by providing two infantry regiments: the *Noúmeroi*, and 'the Regiment of the Walls' or *Teichistai*. These formed the garrison of Constantinople, which – according to the Arab historian and geographer Kudama – totalled about 4,000 men. The first of these two units was responsible for the Imperial prisons located on the site of the ancient Baths of Zeuxippos, called *ta Noúmera*, which flanked the Sacred Palace. Near the Khalké – a spacious and sumptuous building of Constantinian origin – were located the prisons entrusted to the *Teichistai*, who were also responsible for the enclosure of the Sacred Palace. Although not bearing their counterparts' specific title, the *Noúmeroi* also certainly played an important role in the defence of the great Theodosian walls, for a thousand years the ramparts of Constantinople (*De Ceremoniis*, 27, 109).

These regiments were created towards the end of the 7th century, when the members of the city factions who served in the defence of the city began to be considered as permanent troops divided into two *arithmói* (a term with an identical meaning to *noúmeron*). The *noúmeron* on duty in defence of the walls changed its name to *ton Teikhéon*. These units never left the capital, and were responsible for its security if the emperor and the Tághmata were absent. A popular militia also fought beside them, formed by the *Systemata* or associations of craftsmen, merchants and other members of the Circus factions, under the responsibility of the *Éparkhos thes Poleos* (descended from the ancient *Praefectus Urbis*). A third element was provided by the units of urban police in charge of the City Guard, the *Pedatoura* or *Kerketon*. These *milites urbani praesidiarii*, who formed a *taxis* or host, were under the command of an officer called the *Kentyrion*. Sometimes they also acted as an honour escort for the city Eparch.

Officer ranks and appointments

The *Noúmera* and *Teichistai* were organized in the same way. In the *Taktiká* their commander is given, from the reign of Theophilos (r.842–867), the rank of *Dhoméstikos* (or *Kómês* if referring to the *Teichistai*); he had the Imperial dignities of *Anthypatos*, *Patríkios* and *Protospathários*. Under him, in order, came a *Topotêrêtes Spathárokandidatos*, a *Kartoularios*, the *tribunoi*, a *Protomandator*, the *vikarioi*, the *mandátores* and the *portarioi*.

Tribunoi and *vikarioi* were respectively the commanders and vice-commanders of the individual *vánda* within these regiments. In this case, considering that the two regiments totalled 4,000 men, we might guess that the sub-units had a standard strength of 256 men, as given by the *Taktiká* of Leo for the *Vándon-Tághma* (*Diat.* 4, § 56, col. 712). This means that both the *Noúmera* and *Teichistai* should have been composed of about 16 *vánda*. One of the *tribunoi* might have performed the duty borne at the time of Leo I (AD 457) by the *Kómites* of the *Skhólai*, i.e. being charged, in the absence of the emperor, with the military protection of the city. When we read (*De Cer.*, I, 495) of a *Tribounos Preasintalios* who receives the emperor on his return from a victorious expedition, this probably refers to an officer of these troops and not of the *Skhólai*, considering that from the 9th century the rank of *tribounos* is mentioned only in relation to the *Noúmera* and *Teichistai*. We can therefore suggest the hypothesis that this was another aspect of the reforms of Constantine V, who, having transformed the *Skhólai* once more into an effective operational cavalry unit for field employment, had delegated some duties of its officers to units more traditionally linked with the defences of Constantinople.

The sources do not mention standard-bearers of these two regiments, but they probably had the typical *vánda* flags of the Eastern Roman troops. The *portarioi* were charged with the surveillance of the prisons, and they probably carried out the torture and execution of prisoners.

There was a very strict correlation, on the one hand, between the *Noúmera*, the *demoi* of the Blues and Whites (traditionally linked to the court and aristocracy), and the *Tághma* of the *Skhólai*; and on the other hand, between the *Teichistai*, the *demoi* of the Greens and Reds (those associated with the populace and the army), and the *Tághma* of the *Eskoubitores*. Each of the senior *demoi* (the Blues and Greens) was divided into a 'Peratic' faction and an Urban faction, reflecting the two main geographical areas of the city. The *Demarchai* or leaders of the two bigger factions were respectively also the leaders of the smaller political factions of the Whites and Reds.

When organized as militia, the two bigger *demoi* each had a military leader (*Demokrates*) belonging to the Tághmata: the *Dhoméstikos* of *Skhólai*

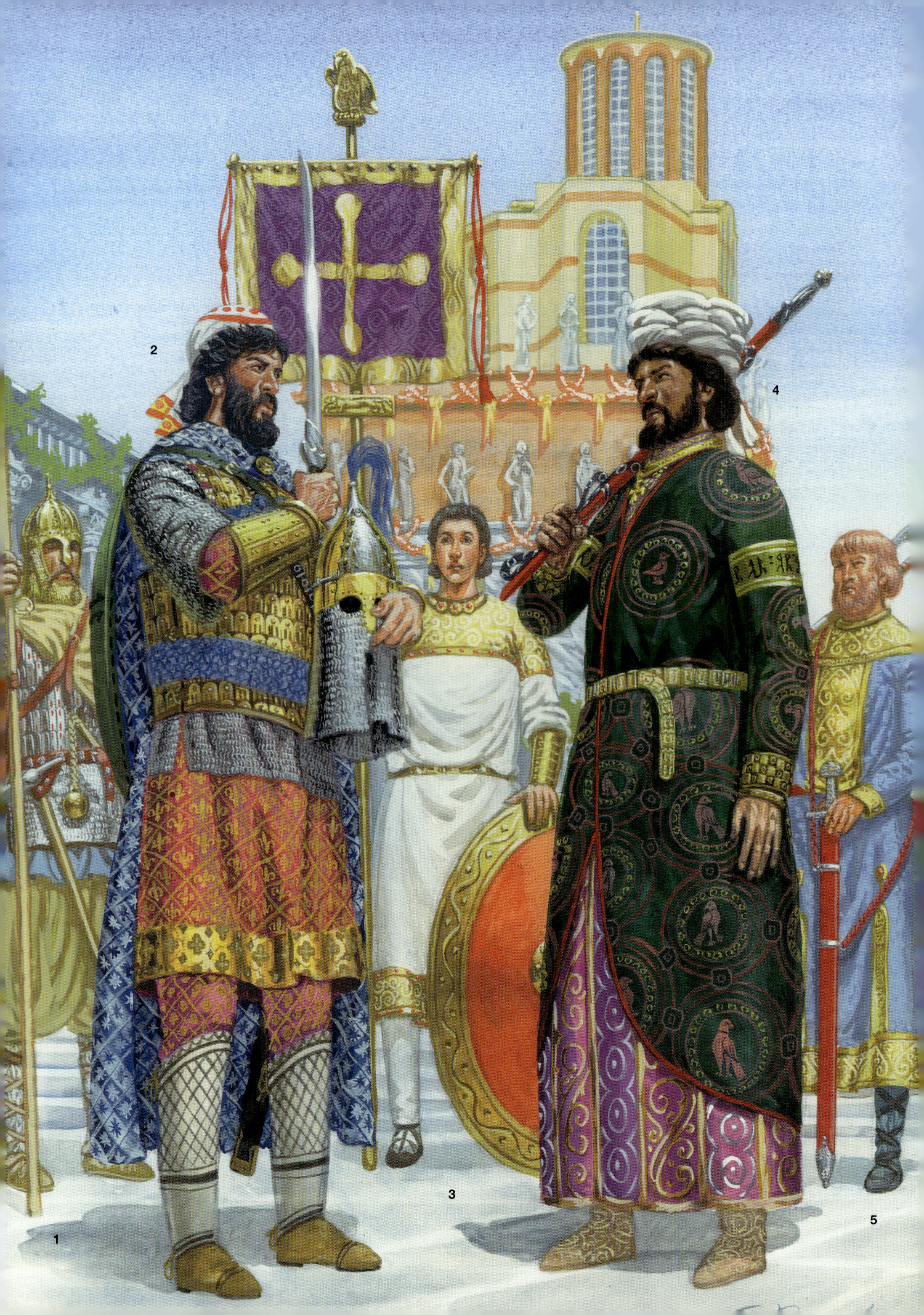
1
2
3
4
5

for the Blues, and that of the *Eskoubitores* for the Greens. Considering that the Blues served with the *Noúmera* and the Greens with the *Teichistai*, those units' direct subordination to the commanders of the most ancient Taghmatic regiments is clear. Formally, therefore, they were parts of the Tághmata, as shown by numerous passages in the *De Ceremoniis*. Indeed, in one passage of that work the writer used the expression *Skhólai* for the Blue faction. This strong relationship was reflected not only in court ceremonial, but doubtless also in the colours of the Palace uniforms (*allaxima*) and in the military clothing of the soldiers (blue and white for *Skholaríoi* and *Noumerarioi*, green and red for *Eskoubitores* and *Teichistai*).

THE *VASILIKOPLOIMON*

The *Vasilikoploimon* was the Imperial war fleet, the maritime equivalent of the Tághmata, of which it carried the troops on great military expeditions. It was a naval Tághma composed of about 12,000 professional warriors manning vessels of high quality, which was at the disposal of the central power. Stationed in Constantinople, where its ships were built and where it had its main harbour, this fleet assured the defence of the capital and of the Thracian coast, from the Propontis to the Pontus Euxinus. However, in the period under consideration here its operations were more often offensive, as the empire tried to restore its territorial integrity.

The typical warship was the bireme *dhrómon*, a long-ship with two banks of at least 25 oars per side in each, giving a total of 100 rowers plus officers, specialists and marines. It is indicated in the 11th–12th century sources by the term *ousiakón khelándion* ('ship with the full crew'). Both *dhrómon* and *khelándion* are employed without distinction to refer to warships by contrast with cargo ships.

Constantine and St Helen. This detail from a miniature of c. AD 880 represents the Eunuch *Spatharokouvikoulárioi*; both they and the *Maghlavítai* of the Imperial Guard were armed with their gold-hilted *spathia* during ceremonies and receptions. The former are shown here carrying them over the shoulder, while the latter wore their swords from the belt. (Cod. Par. Gr. 510, folio 440v; ex Omont)

C — PALACE CEREMONY, 31 MAY 946
1: *Rus* warrior of *Pezetairoi*, fourth *Etaireía*
2: *Protospathários*
3: *Kandidatos*, with Imperial gold *skeptron*
4: *Protokarávos* of the *Vasilikodhrómonion*
5: Imperial *Spathários*

The descriptions given in the original source (*De Ceremoniis*, II, 576–579) are as follows:

'On both the sides of the terrace were lined up the Imperial *Protospathárioi*, wearing *skaramangia* of various colours, green and pink, and their swords **(2)**. And beside them in the next rank stood the *Spathárokandidatoi*, who, girded with their swords, wore multicoloured *skaramangia* and their own uniforms (*spathárokandidatikia*); next were the *Spathárioi*, also with multicoloured *skaramangia* and their swords, and carrying single-bladed axes **(5)**.

'At the door through which you enter the throneroom the *Kandidatoi* were standing **(3)**, with here and there the officers of the *Víghla*, wearing their *skaramangia*, shields and swords... After them were standing... on either side the *Archontogennhematoi*, the *Saponistai* of the *Vestiarion* and the *Ousíai* of the Sacred Dining Hall, wearing, the first, their *skaramangia* and swords; the *Saponistai*, dark tunics; and the personnel of the Dining Hall, light purple garments having short sleeves'.

And finally: 'In the Throneroom of the *Kandidatoi*, behind the bronze doors, in opposed lines, were standing the crews of the *Dhroungários* of the Fleet and of the Prefect of the *Pámphylioi*, holding leather shields (*dorkai*) and wearing their swords' [**(4)** is a deputy commander of one of the warships of the Imperial flotilla] ... standing here and there were other marines... and the baptized Rus **(1)**, who marched on parade with standards, shields and swords of their own land'.

In describing the armament of an offensive *dhrómon* (*meizon dhrómon, khelándion megalon* and *dynatoteron*), Constantine Porphyrogenitus prescribes that the crew should comprise 300 men, 70 of whom are effective fighters – enlisted from the Thematic cavalry regiments and from foreigners or *ethnikoi* – and 230 sailors, some of them also able to fight (*De Cer.*, 670). Leo and Vasilios *Parakoimomenos* inform us that there were *megadhrómones* with about 200 crewmen, 150 of whom were sailors on the upper deck and 50 rowers on the lower deck, but all fighters. In the expedition of 911 against Crete the total crew strength of a *dhrómon* of the Imperial fleet comprised 230 rowers (*kopílatoi*) and 70 fighters (*polemistai*) – in total, 18,000 men for 60 ships. In 949 each of the *dhrómones* of John *Protospathários* had a crew of 220 men, while each of the 20 *dhrómones* of the attacking fleet counted 120 rowers.

The *pamphylos* was a vessel of smaller size – notwithstanding that Leo says that one of these was to be the admiral's flagship, which should fly at least one imperial *flamoulon*. In fact there existed two classes of *pámphylia*. The first or simple *pámphylos* was a rounded cargo ship for carrying military equipment – such as artillery engines – and horses, etc; this was entrusted to a crew of *kopelatoi* (rowers), with a single bank of oars on each side. The *khelándion pámphylion* or *dhrómon pámphylion* was a fighting ship similar to the *dhrómon*, but lighter and easier to handle, with a length of about 65 feet (20 metres).

The terms *pámphyleuo, pámphylon kathistemi* and *poio pámphylon* denote the crews chosen by the supreme commander to man flagships, selected from 'the best soldiers for strength and value and who wear complete war equipment' (Leo, *Tact.*, XIX, 37). A seal of the 10–11th century, published by Schlumberger, confirms that an officer, the *Megas Pámphylos*, was appointed as the Prefect of these *Pámphyloi*, who might be either citizens or foreigners (Italians, Rus, Turks, Slavs, etc). These crews were selected from among the best elements of the Imperial navy, and in the 10th century they formed an elite sea *Tághma* that flanked the Constantinople *Vasilikoploimon*. Essentially this unit formed the naval counterpart of the Imperial Guard *Etaireía* (see below).

Officer ranks and appointments

The command structure of the *Vasilikoploimon* was modelled on that of the *Tághmata*, with officers, who, according to their rank, commanded a certain number of units. The fleet commander, informally called *Stratêgós* in the tactical sources, was officially titled the *Dhroungários ton Ploimon*, classified among the most senior commanders with the rank of *Protospathários* and the dignity of *Anthypatos* and *Patríkios*. He was responsible for the fleet's organization, presided over the councils of war that elaborated strategies and tactics, and checked the weaponry and the appropriate supplying of the ships during a campaign. He had the whole seafront of Constantinople included in the area under his command, and to a large extent he was responsible for the maritime defence of the capital.

This allowed the man in charge to exercise a certain politico-military influence on the central government; indeed, Rhomanôs Lecapênós used his command of the *Vasilikoploimon* as a ladder to the Imperial throne. Presenting himself with the whole fleet in front of the Boukoleon harbour in the year 919, he forced the Emperor Constantine Porphyrogenitus to name him in the Imperial succession. The powers of this appointment were justified by the essential importance of naval defence in the protection of

Constantinople. During three and a half centuries, it was the fleet that saved the capital from seven different sieges; it inflicted serious losses on the Avarian Persians, Arabs and Rus, and the Bulgarians of Czar Simeon could do nothing against the triple walls of Byzantium thanks to the navy's control of the Bosphorus and Golden Horn. In peacetime the *Dhroungários* was responsible for all maritime affairs, a kind of High Commissioner of the Navy.

According to the *Kletorologion* of Phylotheus and the tactical manuals, the ranks below the *Dhroungários* were as follows. A *Topotêrêtes Spatharokandidatos* served as deputy or substitute to the commanding admiral, and other *topotêrêtai* commanded naval squadrons operating far from the capital, such as those of Thessaloniki and of the island of Lemnos. The *Kletorologion* also mentions *tourmarchai* of the fleet, with the status of *Spathárokandidatoi*; these were probably senior officers normally stationed in Constantinople, but who were sometimes entrusted with specific missions in command of the Thematic or provincial fleets (i.e. those naval forces at the disposal of the various regional armies).

A *Kartoularios* was mainly charged with the recruitment of naval personnel (*ploimoi*), but also with the supervision of the fleet's resources. Seals of the 10th century show the ascent up the hierarchy of court ranks of this important personage; at the beginning of the century he has the dignity of Imperial *Spathários*, towards the second half of the century he is already a *Spathárokandidatos*, while at the beginning of the 11th century he has reached the status of *Protospathários*, like that of the fleet commander himself. Alongside him, at least from the 11th century, a *Protonotarios* served as the high treasurer of the Imperial navy, administering the fleet's finances. A seal of the *Protonotarios* Iohannes (published by Schlumberger, p.345) attests that this officer also fulfilled the duties of *Krites* – essentially the 'judge advocate-general' of the navy, presiding over legal disputes between sailors and civilians as well as judging crimes committed by the *ploimoi*.

Next in rank was a *Protomandátor*; and below him were the *kómites* who served as *archontes* (commodores) commanding a naval squadron in addition to their own ship. According to the *Taktiká* of Leo VI, a *kómês* commanded from three to five *dhrómones* with the embarked troops and their *kentarkai*. A squadron thus composed was called a *vándon*, as shown by a 9th-century seal of one Andreas, '*kómês* of the Third *Vándon* of the *Vasilikoploimon*' (published by Laurent, p.538). This rank, as well as that of *Dhroungários*, can be found only among the officers of the Imperial fleet, irrespective of their location. A *kómês* also commanded an *Etaireía* or personal bodyguard of the *Dhroungários*, which might be composed of foreign sailors; this officer belonged to the class of Imperial *Stratóres*.

The *kentarkai* or *ekatontarchoi* (equivalent to the old centurions, and having the dignity of *Spathárioi*) commanded single ships; in the 11th century they were termed *ploiarchai*, with the superior status of *Spathárokandidatoi*. Sometimes the *kentarches* is alternatively identified as a *keubernetes*, or by the more classical title of *trierarches*. The deputy commanders of single ships were termed *protokarávoi* (or, by Vasilios *Parakoimomenos*, also *navarchoi*); Leo prescribes two of them for each ship (*Tact.*, XIX, 8). These officers took command in the absence of the *kentarches*, and some ships were permanently commanded by men of this rank, including the emperor's own two personal *dhromones*.

Junior officers included the *bándophoros* or standard-bearer; Vasilios *Parakoimomenos* calls this officer the *kelevsthes*. The commander was supposed to display 'some flag on his *dhrómon*, a *flamoulon* or *vándon*' (Leo,

Detail from The Judgement of Solomon, a miniature of c. AD 880. We may be fairly confident that the model for this image of a guard, holding the infant and awaiting the king's decision, was a member of the red-uniformed Imperial *Maghlavítai*. The commander of that corps was the 'lord high executioner', who presided over the infliction of corporal punishment, and the death penalty on those judged guilty of treason. For reconstruction, see Plate B1. (Cod. Par. Gr. 510, folio 215v; ex Omont)

Tact., XIX, 39, and see also XIX, 8). The *proreos* was the leader of the armoured boarding party among the crew. In addition there was a musician who played to mark the rhythm for oar movements; in ancient Greek triremes this had been a *trieraules* flautist, but he was now a trumpeter or *voukinator*. *Mandátores* for liaison were also found in the fleet, as were specialist personnel directly under the command of the *Protokarávos*. Each major warship counted among its oarsmen at least one *naupegos*, a kind of naval carpenter able to repair minor damage and oversee the maintenance of the ship.

THE IMPERIAL GUARD

Beside the regiments forming the *Tághmata*, there were four other units constituting an authentic Imperial bodyguard, a kind of 'Praetorian' corps whose members attended upon the emperor at all times – whether he was on campaign, performing the rigid and hieratic protocols of court ceremonial, or even out hunting. Some of these units were formally part of the *Tághmata* – the *Vasilikê Etaireía*, and the marines of the emperor's private Imperial flotilla (*Vasilikodhrómonion*). By contrast, the *Maghlavítai*, and the *Vasilikoi Anthropoi* (literally, 'the Emperor's men'), primarily performed the duties of palace guards and attendants who were entrusted with the protection of the sacred person of the *Vasiléfs*. There were other units of guardsmen who performed ceremonial duties and offices, but who also accompanied the emperor during military operations, such as the *Archontogennematoi*. During the reign of Basil II a further regiment was created that was destined to become the most famous in Byzantium's military history: the *Varangoi*, the Russo-Scandinavian guard of the *Vasiléfs*. All these different units of bodyguards were quartered within the confines of the Sacred Palace in Constantinople.

THE *VASILIKÊ ETAIREÍA*

This regiment of cavalry, 1,000 strong (*Anonymus Vari*, 8), was created in the mid-9th century from a detachment of foreign mercenaries who had fought in the *Vighla* (see above), under the responsibility of the *Akolouthos*. At the beginning its members were called *Hetairoi* (i.e. 'comrades-in-arms' or 'companions'), probably harking back to the tradition of the ancient Macedonian kings as reported by Polybius.

The guardsmen's duties included providing security in the Sacred Palace, but more especially – as their title suggests – they were attached to the person of the *Vasiléfs*, providing him with a personal bodyguard both on campaign and when out hunting. The *flamoulon vasilikon*, the great Imperial banner in silk with gold decorations, was the visible sign of the presence of the *Etaireía* and the emperor.

The regiment was composed of different contingents, called *Etaireíai*, and from the time of Basil I (r. 867–886) until at least 946 there were three main elements. A *Méghali Etaireía* (Great *Etaireía*)

was composed of Macedonians, Christian subjects of the Empire. A *Méshe Etaireía* (Middle *Etaireía*) was associated with the fierce warriors known as *Pharganoi* – Turks from around Ferghanah in Central Asia, and Khazars, a people allied to the Empire who dominated the western Eurasian steppes until defeated by the Rus of Kiev in 965. Finally, a *Mikrhe / Trithe Etaireía* (Small or Third *Etaireía*) was open to non-Christian foreigners; these included Turks and Khazars, Hungarians (Liutprand of Cremona, *Antapodosis*, p.485), Saracens (called '*Agarenoi*' in the sources), and 'Franks' (i.e. Western Europeans). It is likely that the 'Indians' mentioned in the *Liber de Ceremoniis* (I, 234) were converted ex-Muslim negroes who belonged to this latter group of guards. Ibn Rostah, in his *Description of Constantinople*, recalls the presence in the 10th century of Christianized Moors among the palace guards, armed with spears and gold shields.

In addition, the Escorial *Taktikon* (of 971–975) mentions a fourth *Etaireía* composed of infantry (*Pezetairoi*), probably Rus, which is also attested in the *Liber de Ceremoniis* (II, 15, p.579). No doubt *Pharganoi*, Khazars, Arabs, Rus and Franks also served in the Imperial navy. Even when referring to men recruited from the same geographical areas the *Liber de Ceremoniis* often emphasizes a distinction between *ethnikoi* (foreigners) and *vaptismenoi* (baptized). The number of foreign mercenaries increased to such a point that during the 10th century a separate Tághma of *Ethnikoi* was created, under the command of an *Etnarcha*, and at some point the Third *Etaireía* was disbanded.

The mixed recruitment of the *Vasilikê Etaireía* distinguished them from the other Taghmatic units, whose members were found mainly among the Eastern Romans. The foreign mercenary composition of the emperor's bodyguard was a natural consequence of the cosmopolitan character of the Byzantine Empire, with long roots in the old Roman Empire; well paid 'barbarian' Celtic and Germanic guards had been trusted to be immune from Roman factional loyalties. Individual generals also employed similar bodyguards – e.g. the usurper Várdhas Phokás, whose personal guard was composed of Georgians, all equally tall and dressed in 'white armour'. Nevertheless, it was the Macedonian element of the *Etaireía*, men from the same region as the ruling dynasty, who were the most loyal. One of the occasions on which they strenuously defended the throne was in 963, when, under the command of the valiant Marianos Argyros, Macedonian troops of the *Etaireía* opposed the victorious advance of Nikêphóros Phokás on the Bosphorus (Leo Diac., III, 7).

The Great, Middle and Third *Etaireía* were assigned to the command of three *Etaireiárchoi*, while an *Etaireiárchês ton Pezon* ('of infantry')

Detail from miniature, The History of Julian the Apostate, *c.* AD 880. Note (left) the Imperial *Kandidatos* in his white uniform, and the three-knot gold *maniakion* around his neck and falling to his breast. This ceremonial collar is described in the *Kletorologion* of Phyloteus (90–91) as being worn for the investiture of the *Kandidatoi*. The shield is painted red with a gold boss and rim. (Cod. Par. Gr. 510, folio 374v; ex Omont)

commanded the Fourth *Etaireía* (Escorial, 271). The overall commander was the *Méghas Etaireiárchês*, one of the highest dignitaries of the whole Empire, of the class of *Stratarchai* ('generals in chief') and the court rank of *Protospathários*. From 959 this official also received the title of *Patrìkios*, a dignity that was sometimes a stepping-stone to the throne itself – as in the case of Rhomanós Lecapenós, *Méghas Etaireiárchês* in 919 and *Vasiléfs* in 920. The officers of the corps, the *archontes* of the *Etaireía*, were also appointed from among Macedonians (Great *Etaireía*), or partly from *Pharganoi* and *Khazaroi* (Middle *Etaireía*).

Those who procured the title of Guardsmen by bribery or purchase probably belonged to the unit in question only on paper, and it is uncertain whether they accompanied it on active service. The increase of this phenomenon persuaded Haldon to believe that, at the beginning of the 10th century, the unit was turning into a parade body and losing the character of a fighting force. However, the mention of the *Vasilikê Etaireía* about a century later in the *Anonymus de re militari*, which specifies its exact functions and its position during campaigns, suggests that the corps continued to be effective on the battlefield at least until the beginning of the 11th century.

THE *VASILIKODHRÓMONION*

During the late 9th century, under Leo VI, a 1,000-strong Guard naval unit was created. Organized according to the structure of the *Tághmata*, of which it was formally part, this provided the crews of the two luxurious Imperial *dhrómones* from among the emperor's personal flotilla stationed at the capital (see Plate F). Although superbly appointed for use by the sacred Imperial personage, these warships were nevertheless equipped with the terrible 'Greek Fire', the secret projectile incendiary weapon of the Byzantine forces. The sailors of this *Vasilikodhrómonion* also carried about palace tasks, in the ceremonies of the Imperial court, and in monitoring landings at the Boukoleon harbour (*De Cer.*, p. 601). One of the two crews also had to guard the Hippodrome in the absence of the *Víghla* (Constantine Porphyrogenitus, *De administrando Imperio*, 51). These crews, who were combatants as well as seamen, escorted the emperor during his journeys to the sea or to the suburban palaces.

The crews were of mixed composition, including foreigners, especially Dalmatians (*Toulmaltzoi*) and Rus; during ceremonies these always flanked the Eastern Roman sailors (*De Cer.*, II, 579). The sailors who were chosen for this duty were therefore trusted men, and to be included in their number could lead to high promotions. They repeatedly showed their loyalty to the Macedonian dynasty – as when, together with detachments of *Etaireía*, they saved the new Emperor Constantine Porphyrogenitus from the revolt of the *Megas Dhoméstikos* Constantine Dukas (Theoph. Cont., p.383; George the Monk, p.876; Cedrenus, D.280). During the dramatic events that led Nikêphóros Phokás to the throne, an Imperial *dhrómon* was part of the fleet that landed the new emperor at the Hebdomon camp in summer 963 (Cedrenus, p. 250).

The officer in charge of this unit was the *Protospathários* of the Harbour (*tes Phiales*). Each of the two Imperial crews (*ousía dhrómonion*) was commanded by two *protokarávoi* (captains) with the status of *Spathárokandidatoi* – a 'first' captain who was destined to become the *Protospathários* of the Harbour, and a second one (*De Adm. Imp.*, 51). The senior ships' officers, who usually came from the high ranks of the Imperial fleet, are referred to as *protoelatai* ('first

Martyrdom of St Porphyrius, an image of *c.* AD 1000. This detail shows an Imperial *Strator* (right) with his gilded staff (*stratorikion*), wearing his white *phakeolion* head-cloth and a colourful *skaramangion* coat in violet with decorative black, gold and pink-red patterns (compare with Plate B2). His attendant Guardsman (left) wears garments in yellow, gold and scarlet, typical of the magnificent appearance of the Imperial Guard at the time of Basil II. (*Menologion* of Basil II, folio 159, Biblioteca Apostolica Vaticana, Rome; facsimile by Pio Franchi de Cavalieri, author's collection)

among the rowers'), and enjoyed the honour of carrying the Imperial banners (*vasilika flamoulla*) of purple silk and gold that were flown from the two *dhrómones* (*De Cer.*, II, 15, p. 576–577). Their main function was to encourage the rowers, and to assist the *protokarávoi* with the direction of the ship's handling, especially in challenging sea conditions. Next in rank came the *devteroelatai* ('between the second rowers'). On ceremonial occasions these wore the uniforms of the Taghmatics, and carried the *lavara*, *signa* and *kampiduktoria*, as well as flags adorned with gold stripes (*claves*) and other Imperial banners.

In time of war other ships and crews from among the ten-strong Imperial galley flotilla might be incorporated into the fighting fleet, being classified as *supernumerarii* (extra numbers). For the expedition to Crete in the year 949 the Imperial crews deployed included 629 Rus and 368 Dalmatians, and in addition there were – perhaps surprisingly – another 700 ex-prisoner combatants.

TOP LEFT
St George dressed in the uniform of an Imperial Guardsman, in a 10th–11th century fresco from a Cappadocian church; compare with Plate B3. (*in situ*, Church of Aghios Yeorgios, Belisarama; author's photo)

TOP RIGHT
Rather more of the lower part of the Imperial Guard uniform survives in this fresco of St Merkourios from the same site. (*in situ*, Church of Aghios Yeorgios, Belisarama; author's photo)

THE *MAGHLAVÍTAI*

The *Maghlavítai* were ushers, lictors, and imperial mace-bearers (*ravdophoroi/ ravdouchoi Vasilikoi*), who announced the arrival of the emperor in public ceremonies and pageantry. The origins of this body of Palatine guards are very uncertain, and probably not entirely military in character. (Arnold Toynbee's thesis that the term would indicate a body of Western Muslim mercenaries from the Maghreb is without substance.) They may have been established by the Empress Irene (r.780–802) as her personal guard before the creation of the *Víghla*; but their duties and some features of their clothing (see Plate B1) might suggest an uninterrupted descent from the old Roman *lictores*. From the late 8th to the 11th century they formed a small group of attendants on the emperor, equipped with swords, and maces (*ravdoi*) or metal-shod staves (*manglavia*), held as the *lictores* had held their *fascii*. They had 'police' duties, overseeing security and the

D: IMPERIAL ELEVATION OF NIKÊPHÓROS PHOKÁS, AUGUST 963

The scene, set in the Hebdomon camp, is based upon the description in the *Liber de Ceremoniis* (I, 96, 433ff).

1: Emperor Nikêphóros Phokás
The victorious general, known as 'the White Death of the Saracens', wears a *skaramangion kastorion* (i.e. in purple beaver fur), Imperial purple boots (*kokkina podhemata*), and has a single-edged dagger (*akinakis*) at his belt.

2: Kataphraktos of the *Eskoubitores*
This heavy cavalryman of the Tághmata is reconstructed from a steatite plaque representing St Demetrios, today in the Louvre, Paris. He wears a *klivanion* with small scales or *folides*, completely gilded, and reinforced on the left arm by a *zava* formed by *lamellae*. It is worn over a thick, long-sleeved tunic (*chiton*) with embroidered cuffs. His cloak (*chlamys*) is fastened at the right shoulder. From his belt he wears a straight *spathion* with a trilobate pommel, and a kite-shaped shield hangs from his left shoulder.

3 & 4: Kataphraktoi of Imperial Tághmata
Copied from an enamel kept in the St Mark treasury in Venezia, these *kataphraktoi* follow the description in the *Praecepta Militaria* of Nikêphóros Phokás (III, 4, 26–31): 'Each warrior must wear a *klivanion* [which] should have *manikia* down to the elbows. Down from the elbows they should wear *manikelia* [arm-guards]... Both these and the skirts (*kremasmata*) hanging from the *klivania* have *zavai* [protective elements of fabric, sometimes faced with scales or mail] and are made of coarse silk (*koukoulion*) or cotton (*vamvakion*), as thick as can be stitched together'. Note the coloured shoulder tufts, and the rich decoration of the padded over-garment (*epilorikion*) with slit sleeves thrown back **(3)**.

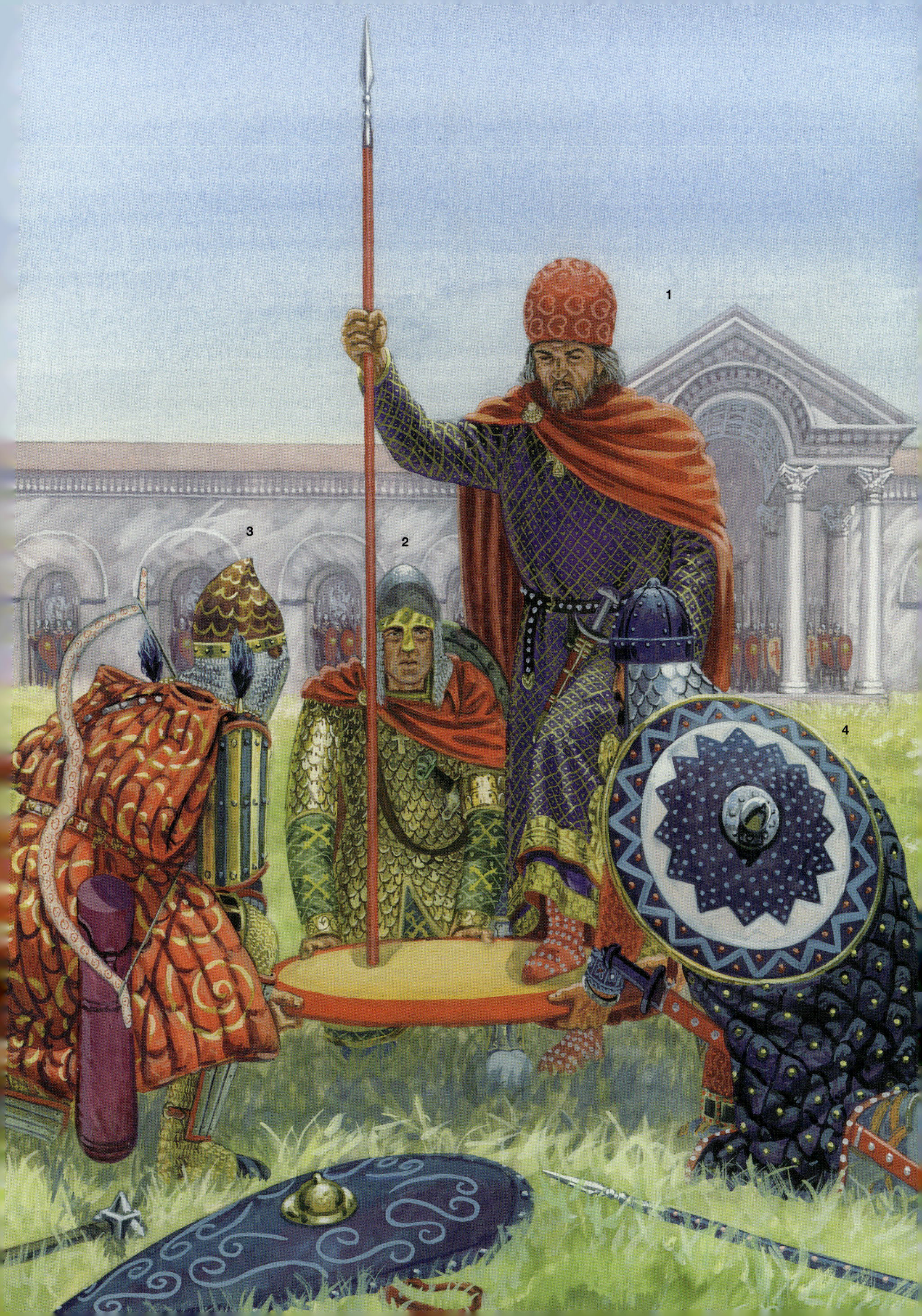
1
2
3
4

maintenance of public order within the Sacred Palace. Their quarters were inside the walls, and their tasks included opening the doors each morning. Together with the *Etaireía*, they preceded the *Vasiléfs* during great public events and opened a way through the crowd with their weapons. Like the *lictores* they had the authority to inflict punishments – even capital, if necessary. Like the *Etaireíoi*, they accompanied the Emperor during hunts and on almost all his travels.

The corps as a whole was generally designated *Manglavion*, subdivided into three classes with the Imperial military status of *Spathárioi*, *Spathárokandidatoi* and *Protospathárioi*. The commander was titled *Primikérios* or *Protomaghlavítes*, but also called simply 'The *Maghlavítes*'; this senior Palace officer had the status of *Protospathários*. When the Guard was on campaign he held the position of *Kómês tes Kortes*, i.e. in charge of the Imperial tent, which the *Maghlavítai* guarded. Sometimes the commander fulfilled special missions on behalf of the *Avtokrator*, notably embassies to vassal and foreign princes taking titles and gifts.

The *Protomaghlavítes* was probably assisted by a vice-commander granted the same dignity or that of *Spathárokandidatos*. We know from Simeon Magister that two such second-rank commanders of *Maghlavítai* were arrested, blinded and exiled for conspiring against the Emperor Rhomanós I in 922, and seals of the 10th–11th centuries recall several officers of the corps holding such a second-level rank. In command of every ten men were *dekanoi*, called *koleteatoi* ('sheath-bearers'), who were also armed with clubs (*De Cer.* I, 81, *Glossae Basilika*). The sources also mention *stratóres* (squires) of the *Manglavion*.

THE *VASILIKOI ANTHROPOI*

These 'Emperor's Men' or 'Imperials' were guard officers of the Palace, who provided the emperor's personal armed escorts and attendants both on the battlefield and at court. At the beginning of the 10th century this Imperial military household comprised: the *Spathárioi*, divided between the two ranks of *Spathárokandidatoi* and *Protospathárioi*; the *Spatharokouvikoulárioi*; the *Kandidatoi* of the Sacred Palace, responsible for the throne-room where ambassadors were received (*Khrysotríklinos*), the Imperial Palace (*Maghnávra*), and the Imperial lodge (*Kathisma*) at the Hippodrome; the *Mandátores* (Imperial messengers); and the *Stratóres* (Imperial squires) under the command of the *Protostrator*, who carried the Imperial *flamoulon* bearing the cross of victory.

The designations of rank were originally related to grades in the personal service of the *Vasiléfs*, and when applied to individuals mentioned in the sources they may equally indicate either effective military appointments or simply honorific titles or dignities granted to mark status at court. For example, the title of *Protospathários*, the highest rank in the *Spathárioi*, carried great importance at the Imperial court and in the Empire, and was awarded to those who occupied senior positions or high commands. In the period under consideration we find various non-military officials holding this title: for instance, the Eparch of the City (*De Cer.*, II, 266), the *Papias* ('Great Doorman') of the Sacred Palace, or the eunuch chamberlain who presided over the personal body-servants of the emperors. But at the same time this title was accorded to men who performed active roles in the *Vasilikoi Anthropoi*; for instance, when the sources mention the *Katalogos Protospathárion* it is clear that they are referring to the military units of the Guard.

In the reign of Theodosius III (r.715–717) the *Spatarii* – so called from the long broadsword that they held (*spatha* or *spathí*) – had originally been eunuch sword-bearers attached to the Imperial person under officers called *Protospatarii*, and from that time their designation was used in a military context. But during the 7th–8th centuries the honorific title of *Spathárokandidatos* also began to be given to senior Imperial attendants with various ranks and dignities. It is very difficult to distinguish in the sources between the various groups of *Spathárioi*: those who were military officers serving as guards, 'adjutants' or staff officers; those who belonged only formally to the unit, but kept their old title as a mark of status after having been transferred; and finally, those serving as active members of the *Spathárioi* unit at court.

When creating the *Tághmata* in the 8th century, Constantine V put them under the command of a *Protospathários* of 'the Imperials' (*Vasilikoi*). The *Spathárioi* therefore kept their importance as staff officers attached to the Imperial person, who charged them with a wide variety of duties, but their significance as a purely military unit would decrease. In a similar way, the *Spatharokouvikoulárioi* were eunuch sword-bearers of the Imperial chambers, attested during the 5th century; they then disappear until mentioned in a source of 869–870, which distinguishes between eunuchs and 'bearded' (i.e. not eunuchs). Their commanders, too, held the rank of *Protospathárioi*, and sometimes the *Spatharokouvikoulárioi* are mentioned in the sources specifically as a *Tághma*, i.e. a military unit.

The *Kandidatoi* were a prominent unit of the Imperial Guard as early as the 3rd–4th centuries, assigned to the protection of the emperor and his *Comitatus*. They were the Palatine unit *par excellence*, selected for their physical appearance and strength, and their title came from their showy white tunic or overgarment (*kandidakion*). Originally, under the Late Roman Empire, there were two groups of *Kandidatoi*, one attached to the VI *Schola* (*Seniores*) and the other to the VII *Schola* (*Juniores*), from which they were selected; each group came under the command of the *Primicerius* of the related *Schola* (*De Cer.* 391, 392). Just 40 of these men formed an escort charged with never leaving the Imperial person, either during ceremonies or when on campaign. From about the mid-7th century this group began to be called *Kandidatoi Vasilikoi*, although their duty was by then more a matter of dignity than an effective armed function.

The army reforms of Constantine V towards the end of the 8th century also involved the *Kandidatoi*. Once again, there would be two groups; but now one would bear the title as an honorary dignity, and one would be an effective fighting unit recruited from among the newly-raised V, VIII and IX *Skhólai*. This latter category would serve full time at the Palace and the Hippodrome (*De Cer.* I, 237). Initially they were left under the command of the *Dhoméstikos ton Skholón*, but in the 9th century they were incorporated into the *Vasilikoi* as a permanent court unit under a separate officer.

Together, the Imperial *Spathárioi*, *Kandidatoi* and *Mandátores* units came under the command of the *Protospathários* of the *Vasilikoi Anthropoi* – the collective designation of this bodyguard corps. Originally titled the *Protospathários* of the Hippodrome (*Taktikón* Uspenskij, pp.842–843), by the year 899 this commander, with supreme responsibility for the security of the Sacred Palace, is already described in Phylotheus's *Kletorologion* as the *Protospathários* of 'the Imperials'. He also began to be called *Katepános*, and belonged to the *Stratarchai* class. From the reign of Leo VI (r.886–912) he was seconded by a vice-commander, the Imperial *Dhoméstikos*.

Joshua and his military retinue, in an 11th-century fresco from Kiev; see reconstruction, Plate H3. This may be the earliest known representation of the Varangians in Byzantine service, since it is contemporary with the founder of the regiment, the Emperor Basil II. The officer (*archon*) in the foreground seems to be wearing leather armour, clearly of Byzantine manufacture. **(Detail:)** the high boot or *hypodhémata*. The device shown in black seems to have been peculiar to the Varangian Guard, and may be a stylization of the emblem of Kiev, whose ruler first sent them to the Emperor Basil's aid. (St Sophia Museum, Kiev; author's photos, courtesy of the Museum)

These Palatine Guards were not limited to performing the complex court ceremonial duties often associated with them, and their military activities are well attested. For instance, 71 'Imperials' took part in the Italian expedition of 935 under Rhomanós Lecapênós (*De Cer.*, 661), and in the same year the Imperial *Mandátores* served in the expedition against Crete (*De Cer.*, 667). They are also remembered on campaign by Liutprand of Cremona: 'a great mob of *Protospathárioi*, *Spathárioi* and *Kandidatoí*' (*De Rebus Europae*, III, 5).

OTHER GUARD UNITS
The *Archontogennhematai*
This word means literally 'the sons of the officers'. These guardsmen were selected from among the youth of the most illustrious Byzantine families, whose fathers had formerly served or were still serving in the Tághmata. They were chosen for their looks and bearing, and performed the role of pages during public ceremonies.

The *Sardoi*
There is a reference in the mid-10th century *Liber de Ceremoniis* to a greeting being sent to the *Vasiléfs* by a particular bodyguard unit called *Oi Sardoi*, probably meaning men from Sardinia. Western elements who were considered to be – at least nominally – Imperial subjects were indeed serving among the cosmopolitan Imperial Guard, especially men from the Italian 'Romanesque' territories (Venice, Gaeta, Naples, Amalfi and Sardinia). The 'Sardians' are recorded by the contemporary Arab historians as brave fighters; the Palermo geographer Edrisi claims that 'the Sardians are different from any other nation of *Rum* [Rome]: they are brave men who never abandon their

weapons.' It is therefore plausible that the Sardoi mentioned in the *Liber de Ceremoniis* were warriors from the ex-Byzantine province of Sardinia, which during the 10th century had not achieved complete independence from Byzantium.

The Varangian Guard

Scandinavian settlers from Russia had served in the Imperial entourage since the time of the Emperor Michael III (r.842–867), and Russo-Scandinavian mercenaries were employed on an *ad hoc* basis from the beginning of the 10th century. The relationship only became formal, however, after 988; in that year Vladimir, Grand Prince of Kiev, responded to a request for troops from the Emperor Basil II by sending 5,000 men south. Their prowess contributed greatly to the emperor's victory over the rebels led by Várdhas Phokás; some of the survivors were formed into a unit of the Imperial Guard, and henceforth the long axes of the Varangians were an unmistakable sign of the emperor's presence on the battlefield. The history and appearance of this unit are covered in detail in a separate Osprey book by the present author and artist: Men-at-Arms 459, '*The Varangian Guard 988–1453*'.

CLOTHING

The tunic (*roukhon*, *chiton*) of the heavy cavalryman might be either a sort of heavy kaftan, fastened with buttons, or the typical sleeved, T-shaped tunic. These could reach down to the knee or even the ankle, and were typically decorated with narrow bands around the wrists.

The three classes of *Spathárioi*, *Spathárokandidatoi* and *Protospathárioi* were distinguished by the kinds of clothing and weapons that they wore during public ceremonies, processions, at the Hippodrome or in the Imperial presence.

Detail from the Joshua fresco, showing (left) the *archon*'s helmet; it resembles simple Late Roman models, but is worn with a white quilted face- and neck-guard. The man on the right, wearing a folded and tied head-cloth, has a red beard – another indication that these are Varangians. (St Sophia Museum, Kiev; author's photos, courtesy of the Museum)

The *allaximata* (*mutatoria*) were precious garments for parade and ceremony that we might term 'Palace dress', as worn by the Guardsmen and Taghmatics on important occasions according to strict court protocols. We should remember that the Eastern Roman hierarchy was composed of hundreds of different ranks, titles and dignities in addition to all the military offices, the army units of infantry and cavalry, and the different bodyguards. Each of them wore its own *allaximata*, although we cannot exactly speak of uniforms in the modern sense. Those of the main Tághmata regiments probably corresponded to the four colours of the city's factions: blue, green, white and red.

Such tunics were furnished with slit or removable sleeves, called *manikia/ manika*; sometimes the material was plain, sometimes embroidered with 'Phrygian' work (the linen so worked was called *avakchevton*). The tunic sleeves might be long or elbow-length (*akromanika* or *kontomanika*). The latter type gave easier movement, and were usually worn with sashes (*loroi*); in the Guard they were reserved to the *Vasilikoi Anthropoi*, but on some occasions the *Eskoubitores* of the Tághmata wore similar short-sleeved tunics with silver and gold embroidery. The officers of the two Constantinople garrison infantry regiments had *kontomanika* with gold bands – *tribounoi* in green or blue, and *vikarioi* in green and red. These were *chrysoshementa* – tunics ornamented with silk bands covered with gold thread, applied at the ends of the short sleeves and at the bottom edge of the skirt.

Clothing items that formed types of *allaxima* were termed *skaramangia*, *stemmata*, *loroi*, *chlamyda* and *divithisia*. The primary court dress was the *skaramangion*, the 'dress uniform' of the Eastern Roman cavalry. It was a true horseman's kaftan, adopted by the Late Romans from Perso-Caucasian models. Gradually it had become a garment characteristic of officers and commanders, and then, due to its widespread use by dignitaries during the 9th–10th centuries, this military garment evolved into court dress. The Imperial Guardsmen had *skaramangia* of various colours and cuts. The *skaramangia prasinodina* were reserved for the *Protospathárioi*; such garments were made in double colours, green and pink. Other *skaramangia* were woven in very thick thread with figures of animals, of Sassanian inspiration. During ceremonies the Guardsmen were drawn up to form groups dressed in a similar way: 'Each of the various kinds of *skaramangia* had its designated place: the green and pink eagles here, the oxen and the [?] eagles there, the bowls here, the white lions there' (*De Cer.*, II, 578). Each regiment and officer rank of the Tághmata had its own *skaramangion*, worn for certain prescribed feasts and ceremonies.

The military mantle, the *chlamis*, was mainly of white for the four Tághmata, but all the four colours of the Circus factions are mentioned in *De Ceremoniis*.

WEAPONS & EQUIPMENT

Research concerning the weapons and military equipment used in the Eastern Roman empire, previously based mainly on textual references and depictions in frescoes and other pictorial sources, has now been supported by archaeology. In recent decades artefacts have been recovered not only in the former territory of the empire – especially Bulgaria and Turkey – but also in the lands from which the Byzantines recruited the best mercenaries for their army. (These last were significant among the Imperial troops: for example, the

500 Taghmatic Armenians of Platanion, who fought in Crete in 911, were described as 'the most skilled soldiers and expert archers and, if possible, some of them even the best trained cavalrymen, both among the officers and among the simple *Skholárioi*' – *De Cer.*, 658.)

WEAPONS
Swords

The sources tell us that in the 9th–10th centuries enough iron was stored in Constantinople to make 4,000 sword blades every year (*De Cer.* 674, 3). Various names are used for bladed weapons, but especially *xiphos* and *spathi*. The sword was carried in a scabbard (*thekarion*, or *kouleos* – Achmet, 114, 12–14), often made of leather, willow wood, or sometimes both.

The long, straight *spathion*, descended from the Late Roman *spatha*, is the commonest type seen in the iconography. Its average length was between 33 and 45in (85–115 centimetres). The total length of cavalry swords, hilt included, was to be 'not less than 4 spans' (*Sylloge Tacticorum*, XXXIX, 2). A span was 12 fingers or say 9in (23.4cm); so a cavalry sword of *c*. AD 900 was at least 36in (91.4cm) in total length. According to the *Sylloge*, the *kataphraktoi* carried both a double-edged sword hanging from a baldric, and a single-edged sword slung from the belt and called for this reason a *paramerion*. Other treatises also attest this use of two swords: 'they should moreover be equipped with swords, worn from the shoulders in the Roman way, and *paramíria*, i.e. swords at the belts' (Leo, *Tact.*, VI, 2). According to the *Praecepta Militaria* of the Emperor Nikêphóros Phokás, each cavalryman should have a sword – the *kataphraktoi*, two – plus a spear, mace or bow (*Praec. Mil.*, XII, 10–12, XIII, 31s, XII, 23–26).

The light and heavy infantry wore the double-edged sword slung from the waist belt (*paramerion* or *spathion zostikion*), with a total length of 4 spans (*Syll. Tact.* XXXVIII, 5, 7, 10; *Praec. Mil.* I, 24s., II, 11). However, judging from the sources, the term *paramerion* might sometimes indicate a single-edged curved sabre, probably associated with the presence of the *Pharganoi* Turks and Khazars in the Imperial Guard from the second half of the 9th century.

The sword pommel might be spherical, half-spherical, lenticular, oval, rosette-shaped, pear-shaped, onion-shaped, half-moon shaped, a flat disk, trefoil or ring; hilts were of metal, wood, bone or ivory, sometimes wrapped with cord or copper-alloy wire. A small ring was sometimes set in the pommel in order to attach a wrist strap, from which the sword might hang; this strap was sometimes decorated with a small tuft or *thouphion*. During the 10th–11th centuries the quillons of the crossguard became longer, and might curve downwards; in some cases they terminated in small spheres. Sword blades were

Gilded pommel of 10th-century Byzantine sword found during excavations at Abritus, Bulgaria. (Photo courtesy Prof Valeri Yotov)

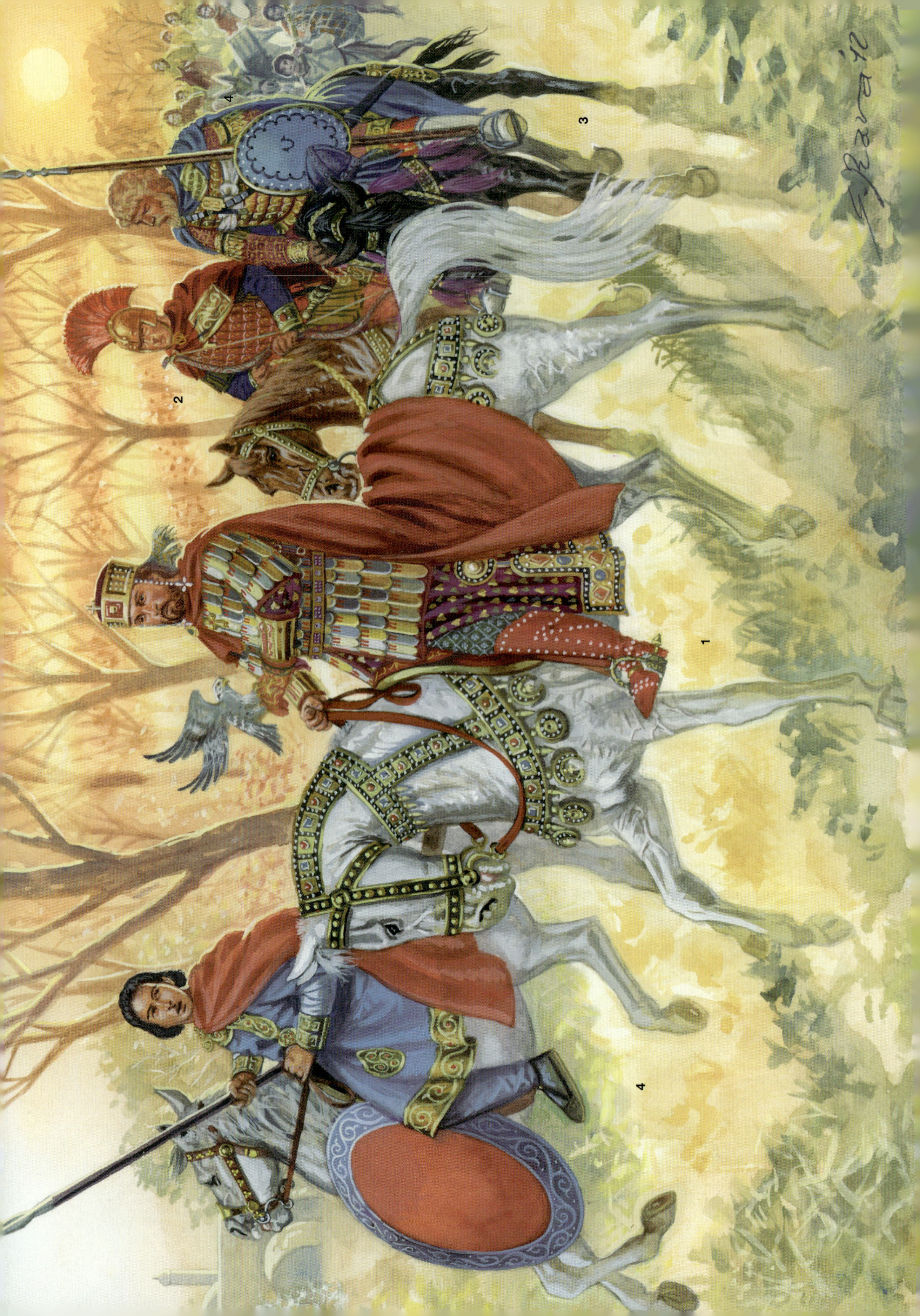

1
2
3
4
4

usually thick, with a central fuller, but Persian influence could also be seen in some thinner, more elegant blades.

Archaeological finds in recent decades have helped to establish a typology of swords and their details as produced inside the territories of the Empire and in neighbouring countries in the 10th to 11th centuries. For instance, swords from Tekija (Kladova, Serbia), Cierny Brod and Jarohnvice (Slovakia), Kunagota (Hungary), Sfintu Gheorghe (Romania), and Ostrov (Bulgaria) have now been identified by Professor Valeri Yotov as 9th–11th century weapons made in the territory of Byzantium. Additionally, many sword guards and chapes recovered from Pliska and Kaskovo (Bulgaria), Chersonesus (Ukraine), Pacului Soare (Romania), Serçe Limani (Turkey), and from Syrian and Iranian sites – these last probably war-booty, decorated by Muslims with Kufic and Koranic inscriptions – can be identified as 10th–11th century pieces of Byzantine origin. All of them have parallels in Byzantine manuscript illustrations, church frescoes, and ivory or stone reliefs showing Imperial Guardsmen.

A clear characteristic of one type of 9th–11th century sword is a sleeve-like projection below the crossguard, extending for approximately an inch (2–3cm) down the blade. This is visible on the Kunagota grave 1 sword, and is similar to swords shown in – among others – the 10th-century Hosios Loukas fresco of Joshua. Professor Yotov suggests a mid-10th century date for this type, and a sword found underwater at Serçe Limani gives grounds to believe that similar sword guards were still in use in the first half of the 11th century.

The Imperial Guardsmen often carried special, decorated swords. Beyond its practical purpose, the sword became a symbol of power and an Imperial insignia, carried as a mark of rank by some courtiers, dignitaries and the emperor's relatives, as well as by distinguished officers of the Palatine units. Swords were carried unsheathed during ceremonies by Guardsmen – the

Early 9th-century Byzantine sword found during World War II in a trench near Suhaya Gomolsha village in the Kharkov region of Ukraine. Note the sleeved extensions above and below the crossguard – the latter is not part of the scabbard. (Private collection; photo courtesy Prof Valeri Yotov)

E: IMPERIAL LION-HUNT, SYRIA, c. 975
Lion-hunting was a favourite sport of the young sons of the Anatolian aristocracy, and a good preparation for war.

1: Emperor Iohannes Dzimiskés
The emperor – who in 969 replaced Nikêphóros Phokás in the affections of the dowager Empress Theophanó, and on the throne – is reconstructed here after Leo the Diacon's description of his gilded armour, and his portrait in the Cappadocian church of Cavusin. Note the alternating lacquered iron and gilt bronze *lamellae*, and the gilded splint-armour *manikelia* on his forearms. His horse harness is based on the emperor's horse shown on the Troyes casket.

2: Macedonian *kavallarios* of the Great *Etaireía*
This Macedonian cavalryman of the elite 'Imperials' is also based on the Troyes casket. The use of horn plates for some *klivania* is attested by the written sources, and by archaeological finds in Bulgaria. The dimensions of these *petala* and the red-lacquered finish are from 11th-century miniatures. The sword is from the Serçe Limani specimen. Note his powerful composite bow.

3: Cavalryman of the *Athanatoi*
This member of the èlite Taghmatic regiment, 'the Immortals', is from the *Menologion* of Basil II. The gilded *klivanion* is of typical banded lamellar construction with central rivets, and the *kremasmata* lappets of the lower border are silvered. The white command-rank sash (*loros*) is probably of silk. The light blue *chlamys* has a splendid ornamented *tablion* in gold thread (see also **2**). The richly decorated dark red trousers (*anaxyrida*) show a pattern of gold circlets between gold vertical stripes, and are tucked inside white and cerulean *kampotouvia*. The spear has a silvered head and a globular terminal. The light blue shield (*cheiroskoutarion*) has a gilded rim and is decorated with white dots, in imitation of pearls. The *spathion* is carried in a black scabbard with light blue fittings.

4: *Archontogennematos*
The blue uniform of this aristocratic young officer shows his family's strong connections with the 'Blues' – one of the four socio-political factions associated with the Circus in Constantinople. The style of decoration of his *allaxima*, with *clavi et orbiculi*, is still identical to that of the Late Roman Empire.

BELOW
10th-century Byzantine iron sword found on the site of the fortress of Kotel, Bulgaria. Although some scholars propose an earlier date, its striking similarity to a 10th-century sword from Tekjia seems to point to a similar chronology. (Local museum, Kotel; photo courtesy Prof Valeri Yotov)

Pharganoi and *Khazaroi* of the *Etaireía*, the officers of the *Víghla*, the *Archontogennematai*, the *Méghas Pámphylos* and the marines of the Imperial Fleet, and the Dalmatian and Rus sailors (*De Cer*. II, 576–579). However, the tales of Leo the Diacon about the deeds of Theodosius Mesonytes, Anemas Kouroupas and Konstantinos – members of the Imperial bodyguard of Iohannes Dzimiskés – also stress the terrible effectiveness of the swords of the Imperial Guard on the battlefield (Leo Diac., VIII, 6; IX, 6; VI, 12–13).

RIGHT
Two views of a 10th–11th century sword guard from Pliska, the first capital of the Bulgarian kingdom. Again, note the characteristic sleeve-like extensions. (Photos courtesy Prof Valeri Yotov)

44

Daggers

Daggers were widely employed. During a hunting party the future Emperor Leo VI, having in mind an attempt on the life of his father Basil I, wore a *machairion* short enough to be hidden inside his boot. The *Sylloge Tacticorum* (XXXIX, 5) recommends heavy cavalrymen to wear a *machairion* attached to the quiver straps. Archaeology confirms the iconography – especially in the *Menologion* of Basil II – showing the employment of short knives, with a long, curved handle corresponding to about two-thirds of the length of the blade. The word *akinakis* indicated a short Persian-style blade, for the Eastern Romans a kind of dagger worn at the belt – for instance by Nikêphóros Phokás, when he addressed his soldiers (Leo Diac., 41, 21–23).

ABOVE
Head of a cast iron 9th–10th century Byzantine war-mace, with a quadrangular arrangement of 'wings' or flanges. (World Museum of Man, Florida; photo courtesy John Macnamara)

BELOW
Head of 10th–11th century Byzantine mace, with spiral flanges. (World Museum of Man, Florida; photos courtesy John Macnamara)

Spears

In this period, the word *arma* usually indicated spears and shields, with particular reference to those carried by the Imperial Guard; indeed, the emperors themselves did not disdain to carry these on some ceremonial occasions.

The Late Roman heavy armoured cavalryman had always been equipped with a long lance, and Byzantine tactical manuals mention the need for him to be provided with two. One unit, the *Kontaratoi*, was even named after its main weapon; this long *kontarion* was wielded on horseback using both hands (Leo Diac., VI, 11). The spears used by the Imperial Guard were mainly of ash (*melia*) or cornel (*krania*) wood. They were 8–10 cubits long, i.e. between about 12ft 4in and 15ft 5in (3.75–4.7m), the longest reaching 20ft 5in (6.25 metres). According to the *Sylloge Tacticorum* and Leo VI's *Taktiká*, the *dorata* of the heavy infantry and the 'small' throwing *kontaria* measured 12ft 4in with heads just over 9in long (3.75m & 23.4 centimetres). Most spearheads were of iron, but there were also examples in bronze, and parade specimens finished in gold and silver. The iron-shod spear butt or ferrule was widely used, especially among the infantrymen (*Praec. Mil.*, V, 3).

Cavalry spears were often fitted with small flags attached by means of rings, which may have distinguished different units by their colours and shapes. They might be shaped like pennants (*flamoula*), or as small squares or rectangles with streamers (*vánda*). The manuals tell us that before battle the flags were taken off the spears and kept in special cases (*thekaria*), so that the spearmen and the archers behind them were not distracted by them.

The Imperial spears were costly, richly decorated ceremonial pieces. Golden spears – i.e. with gold or gilded heads, or gold-plated wooden shafts – were borne in triumphal parades. The sources often describe richly ornamented spears, such as the two silver spearheads decorated in gold preserved in the Sanctuary of St Theodore in the *Khrysotriklinos* (throneroom) of the Palace, and one even mentions a spear decorated with pearls. During processions the *Spathárioi* bore the emperor's weapons, including his spear.

Maces

The *sidiroravdion* (or simply *ravdion*) was the war-mace used, according to 10th-century tacticians, by both Taghmatic infantry and cavalry (*Praec. Mil.*, I, 1, 25; III, 7, 54–57; Nikêphóros Ouranós, 56, 29; 60, 69, 84: 61, 211).

F | BOUKLEON HARBOUR, 10th–11th CENTURIES

1: *Proreos* of Imperial *Ploimoi*
This officer commands the armoured boarding party among the crew of one of the warships of the Imperial flotilla. The best examples of ringmail corselets (*lorikia psilà*), with bronze, gilded or silvered rings, were reserved for officers and soldiers with special duties. The *Liber de Ceremoniis* mentions a restricted number being available to *dhrómon* crews in addition to the 'common' *lorikia koinà* (*De Cer.*, II, 669–670). Note also the masked helmet (*kassidion avtoprosopon*), and the leather shield (*dorka*), based respectively upon the Great Palace finds and the *Menologion* of Basil II.

2: *Kentyrion* of *Pedatoura*
The old-fashioned 'muscled' armour of this officer of the Constantinople 'urban police' or City Guard can be explained by his traditional position in the command hierarchy of the city *Éparkhos*. Some officers' helmets were covered with oriental ornamentation, and perhaps by a hood of woven silk and costly damask. David Nicolle has observed the clear derivation of that type of headgear (*kamelaukion*) from Alan-Caucasian prototypes.

Background: Imperial *dhrómon*
The flotilla of the *Vasiléfs*, which was used by the court at Constantinople on official religious and secular occasions, was composed of three categories of vessels: red and black pleasure craft (*agraria*); ten warships (*khelándia* or *dhrómonia*) stationed on the Bosphorus; and two large *dhrómonia* that Leo VI had turned into 'luxury yachts' – the *Vasilikos Dhrómon*, and a second ship called the *Akolouthos* ('Follower').

1

2

It usually had an iron head mounted on a wooden shaft, although there were also examples made entirely of iron, with sharply-angled flanged heads. The mace was prescribed as a close-combat weapon for the heavy cavalry *kataphraktoi*, capable of crushing in helmets, armour, and even horses' skulls. It was carried as their sole shock weapon by all heavy cavalrymen in the first four lines of their battle formations. Leo the Diacon tells us of one Theodore Lalakon, who 'slew a great many of the foe with an iron mace (*sidhera koryni*); bringing it down with the might of his hand, he shattered both the helmet and the head encased within it' (Leo Diac., 144–145).

According to the *Praecepta Militaria*, both maces and swords or sabres were the shock weapons of the cavalrymen of the Imperial Tághmata (*Praec. Mil.*, IV, 6–7). This source stresses the employment of the mace by cavalrymen, mentioning that the light cavalry or archers placed within the formations of the *kataphraktoi* could be armed with maces as well as swords and lances (*Praec. Mil.*, III, 9, 70–72). The heavy cavalrymen might carry the mace in three different ways: in a sheath attached to their saddle (*Syll. Tact.*, XXXIX); at their belt (Theophanes Continuatus); or by means of a strap or cord around the wrist (Leo the Diacon). '[The cataphracts] should have their iron maces and sabres in their hands and have other iron maces either on their belts or saddles' (*Praec. Mil.*, III, 7, 57–60).

Both the iconography and the archaeology allow us to distinguish various shapes for the maces used in this period. Polygonal heads might be of triangular, squared, hexagonal, octagonal, winged or flanged designs. Round heads might be simple, flanged, spiked or knobbed. 'The *Kataphraktoi* should have... iron maces with iron heads – the heads must have sharp corners and be three-cornered, four-cornered, or six-cornered – or else other iron maces' (Nikêphóros Ouranós, *Taktika*, 60.66ff; the general uses the word *olosidira*, to indicate specifically all-iron maces rather than wooden-shafted weapons). Round-headed spiked maces are shown in the iconography carried by both infantrymen and cavalrymen, but especially in the hands of officers, nobles and guardsmen.

Axes

Guardsmen might carry either double-bladed or single-bladed axes. The axes with double blades (*bipennes*) were commonly called *pelekis*. The single-bladed were called *distralion monopelukon* or *monopeluka*, and the *Liber de Ceremoniis* informs us that they were issued to the Macedonians of the *Etaireía*. 'The *Spathárokandidatoi* are carrying... their shields and their single-edged axes; the *Spathárioi* their shields and their axes, both dressed in the *skaramangion*'; and 'they are standing on both sides, carrying their *distralia*' (*De Cer.*, I, 148; I, 72). These axes were called *distralia* specifically because they were carried by the Guardsmen not with the left hand, like the spear, but with the right hand. So during ceremonies the *Dhroungários thes Víghles* carried, in addition to his sword and a club (*manglavion*), his axe (*tzikourion*) resting on his right shoulder (*De Cer.*, II, 524).

11th-century Byzantine battleaxe head from Bulgaria, measuring 6.7in × 11.8in (17 × 30cm). This shape is often seen in artworks of the period. (Photo courtesy Prof Valeri Yotov)

The term *eteropelekis* refers to pole-axes with a blade shaped like a half-moon. The *spathovaklia*, later called *rhompaia*, were a particular kind of pole-arm issued to bodyguards. They consisted of a long wooden shaft mounting a long, single-edged blade at the end, this sometimes taking the shape of a scythe. Constantine Porphyrogenitus speaks of the *Protospathárioi* with swords and *spathovaklia* 'resting on their shoulders'.

Bows

Due to the influence of the Euro-Asiatic peoples, from the Late Roman period bows and arrows had become an essential element of Roman equipment, especially for the cavalry. The word indicating the complex of the bow and its equipment is *toxopharetra* (a bow and a quiver with arrows). At the beginning of our period the heavy cavalry *kataphraktoi* were generally lancers, but archers (*sagittarioi*) were also present in their ranks – approximately 40 per cent of them were mounted archers. Archers were an integral part of both the infantry and cavalry of the Taghmatic forces, and according to the *Praecepta Militaria* they made up about 25 per cent of the infantry.

The powerful reflex-curved composite bow, inherited from the Steppe peoples, had a maximum flight range – not an accurate battle range – listed at 156 *orguiai* (359 yards/ 328.4m) for infantry archers, and 142–147 yards (130–135m) for mounted archers. According to the *Sylloge Tacticorum* (XXXIX, 4) this bow was 15–16 *palaistai* long (3ft 9in–4ft 1in/ 1.17–1.25m), smaller and less tightly strung for the cavalry than for infantry archers. A single quiver usually held 40–50 arrows. The infantry formations had skilled light archers (*psiloi toxotai*) of whom 4,800 carried two quivers (*koukoura*) each, one with 40 arrows and the other with 60; they had two bows each, and four spare bowstrings (*Praec. Mil.*, I, 4; also Nikêphóros Ouranós, *Taktika*, 56.4). In addition to the arrows that they supplied themselves, the archers in each Taxiarchy received another 50 from the huge stocks of 'Imperial arrows' (*Vasilikai sagitai*).

The Eastern Roman archers knew both the Mongolian draw, in which the bowstring was pulled back by the thumb (usually protected by a ring, often found in the excavations) supported by the index and middle fingers; and the Mediterranean draw, in which the archer used the top three fingers to draw the bowstring while holding the arrow between the index and middle fingers. Leo the Diacon (50, 21s.) describes the Emperor Nikêphóros Phokás drilling his Guardsmen 'to draw the bow flawlessly, to bring the arrow back to the chest and shoot directly at the target'. These exercises were performed in the Circus (Hippodrome) of Constantinople; representations of Imperial Guardsmen performing displays in the Circus and training with bow, shield and spear are found on the frescoes of St Sophia in Kiev. Leo the Diacon compares the archery skills of the Emperor Iohannes Dzimiskés favourably with that of the legendary Odysseus, claiming that he could shoot an arrow through a finger ring (Leo Diac., 96–97).

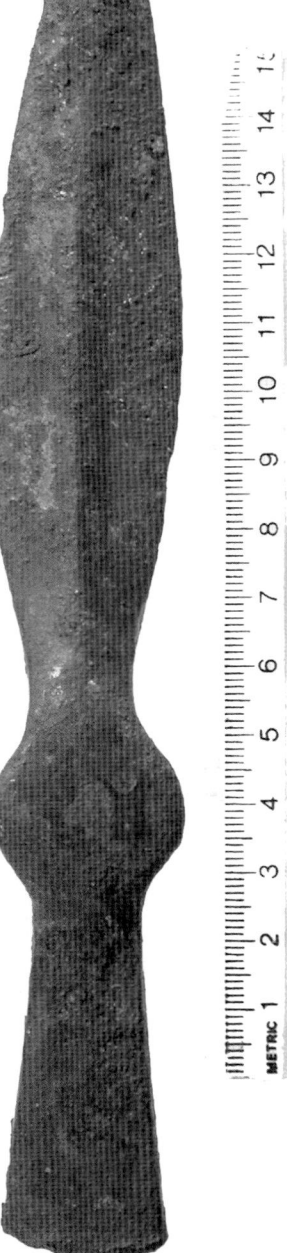

Found in Bulgaria, the head of a 10th-century *akouphion* or war-hammer, seen from end-on. According to the writings of Leo the Diacon, the Emperor Nikêphóros Phokás was killed with such a weapon by Iohannes Dzimiskés. (Photo courtesy Prof Valeri Yotov)

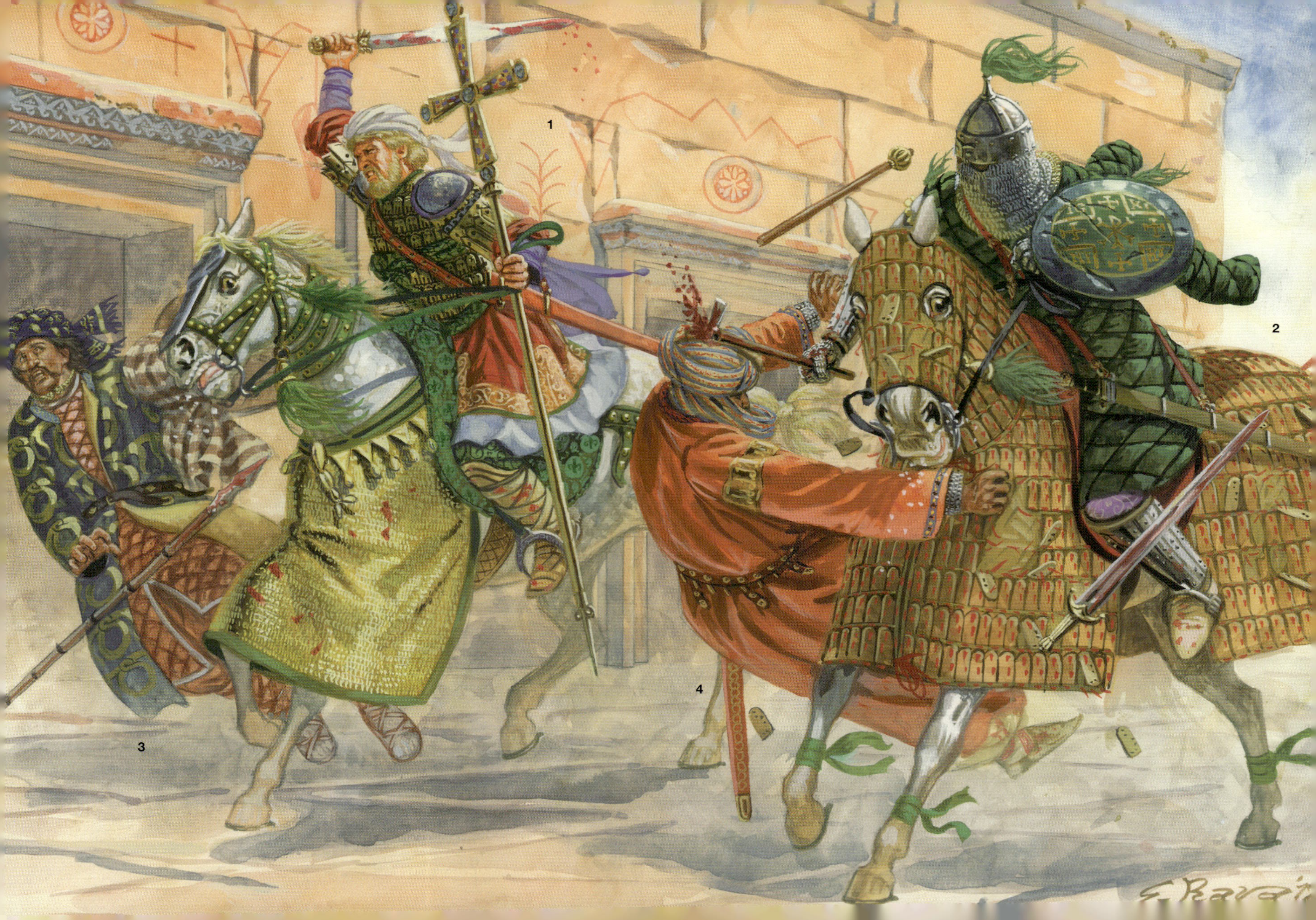
1
2
3
4

Archer's thumb ring, 11th century, found near Strumica in Macedonia. (Photo courtesy Prof Vane Sekulov, Strumica Museum)

DEFENSIVE EQUIPMENT
Helmets

Helmets (*perikephalaia*, *kranos*, *korys*, *kassidia*) were usually made of iron, but the sources also attest the existence of other headpieces constructed from leather, felt or other fabric.

In those illustrations that certainly or plausibly represent Guardsmen the helmets are shown as either basically hemispherical, or of conical pointed shape (*Codice Vathopedis* n. 760). The first type represent the evolution of Late Roman models. A pointed helmet found in southern Russia, identical to those represented on Imperial infantrymen in the Psalter of Basil II, has been classified by scholars as a Byzantine piece of the 11th century.

G: GUARDSMEN IN ACTION, 995

1: *Proximos* of Imperial *Skhólai*
This important staff officer of the senior *Tághma* is based upon a portrait dated to 1007, of Iohannes, a *Proximos* with the court rank of *Protospathários*, who served under the *Dhoux* Theodorakan in the Théma of Armenia. Note his gilded *klivanion*, and the cross standard.

2: Imperial *Kataphraktos* with armoured horse
The texts also refer to the heavy armoured cavalryman of the *Tághmata* as a *kavallarios* or *klibanophoros*, but they are unanimous in their lists of the protective elements that he needed to wear on his upper body (see commentary to Plate D). Nikêphóros Ouranós (60, 4, 39–40) differs from the *Praecepta Militaria* only in calling the forearm protection *cheiropsella*. Note the use of the war-hammer (*akouphion*) as an alternative 'shock weapon' to the mace for the ranks given the task of breaking into enemy formations.

3 & 4: Egyptian Fatimid warriors
Based upon a plate now in the Victoria & Albert Museum, London, and the Louvre plaque in Paris. According to Byzantine sources, some Fatimid infantry wore pink fabric 'soft armour', probably quilted.

RIGHT
Helmet from Yasenovo, probably Byzantine, 11th century. The date is debatable, and some scholars have identified it as of Mongolian rather than Byzantine origin. However, it is identical to one shown worn by an 11th-century Imperial Guardsman in the Barberini Psalter, folio 84v. (Kazanlik Regional Museum; author's photo, courtesy the Museum)

BELOW
A gilded helmet nasal guard of c. AD 1000 from Constantinople. This extraordinary piece – published here through the courtesy of the Director of the Istanbul Archaeological Museum – was recently recovered during major excavations of the area of the harbour of Theodosius, which yielded more than 66,000 items relating to the material culture of Byzantium between the 4th and 11th centuries. The fact that this nose-guard was completely gilded suggests that it belonged to an officer of the Imperial fleet or the Imperial Guard. (Istanbul Archaeological Museum Depot; photo courtesy Dr Zeynep Kiziltan)

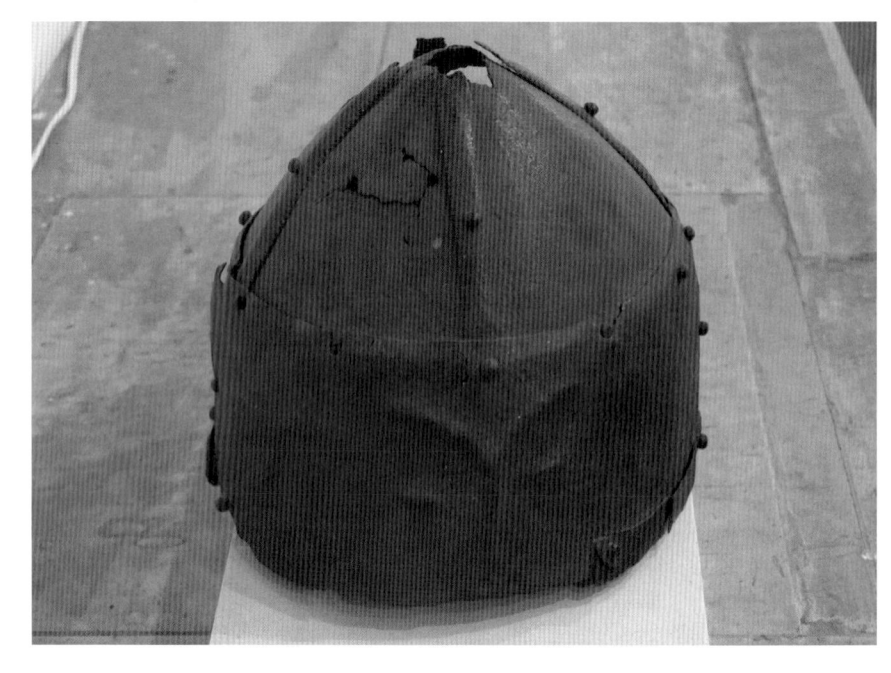

The most widely seen helmets are straight-edged above the eyes and ears, often with attached protection for the ears and neck; this is usually an *aventail* made of leather or fabric strips, or of interlocking scales or rings. Helmets of fully armoured cavalrymen (*pansideroi ippotatoi*) were more compact, and fitted with protection for the face. The sources speak of 'complete' helmets (*korytes teleiai*) worn by heavy infantrymen and *kataphraktoi*, and 'incomplete' helmets worn by light cavalrymen (*kranos* – 'bowl helmet'), depending upon whether or not they were fitted with face protection. Some helmets had clearly evolved from the simplest types of Late Roman *spangenhelm*, quick and inexpensive to make. This may explain how in 963 the former *Parakoimomenos* Vasilios was able to equip 3,000 of his servants to attack the estate of one Joseph Bringas with these helmets, felt caps, *thorakes* body armour, small round shields, javelins and swords.

A single source may perhaps indicate Byzantine use of masked helmets: the *Liber de Ceremoniis* mentions, in addition to the 80 *kassidia* issued for the crew of a *dhrómon*, ten '*kassidia avtoproposopa*' – perhaps intended for the *protokarávoi* and *proreis* officers. During excavations of the Great Palace in 1953, on the marble floor of one room were found nine iron masks, about 7in (18cm) long, with holes for the eyes but not for the mouth, and with small pairs of fastening holes at the top and in the middle of each side. The fact that they were all of iron, had no mouth holes, were found together, and were very close in number to those mentioned in *De Cerimoniis* for the issue to a warship's officers, might suggest that they were battle masks for attachment to helmets. Their shape recalls the mask visors of helmets still visible on the fragmentary 5th-century Columns of Theodosius and Arcadius, and also that of the 7th-century Sutton Hoo

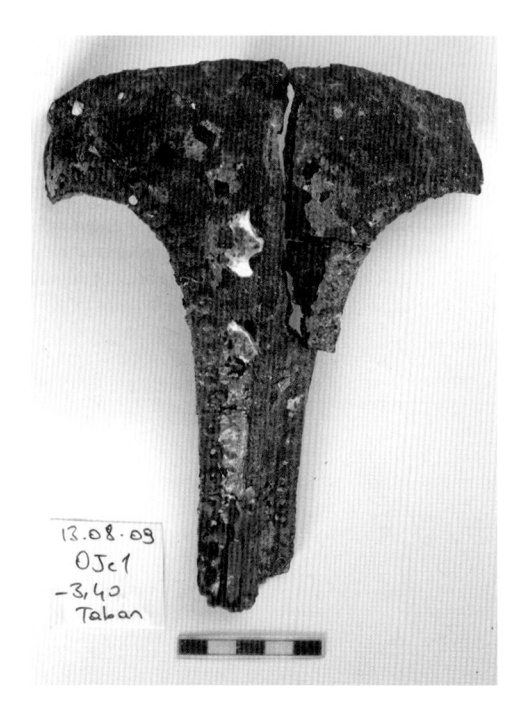

LEFT
Some of the nine iron helmet masks found in the Great Palace of Constantinople during the 1953 Talbot Rice excavations. These 10th-century pieces, pierced for the eyes but not the mouth, are discussed in the text, page 52. The scale line at the bottom of the photo is marked in centimetres. (Courtesy DAI Library)

helmet from Britain, which shows Late Roman influence. Intriguingly, the passage from Constantine Porphyrogenitus's book also suggests that the *kassidia avtoprosopa* were supplied to *Siphonatores* – the operators of the main Greek Fire projecting machine or *katakorax*.

According to the *Praecepta Militaria*, the helmets of the *kataphraktoi* were of solid iron, with two or three layers of ringmail covering the face so that only the eyes remained visible. The rings were sewn to a fabric base, either forming a hood or attached to hang from the edges of the helmet. It is possible that scales were sometimes used instead of ringmail. A ringmail hood (*skaplion*) could be attached to the collar of body armour.

The *peritrachelion* is mentioned only by Leo (*Taktika*, V, 4); it is described as circular, with an outer fringe of linen and a wool lining (*endedymena*), and covered externally with scales or rings. These details suggest that *peritrachelia* were worn around the neck, reaching up to the helmet and with a flap hanging partly over the chest, ending with a border of fringes. The *Codex Ambrosianus* (139, B119 sup) informs us that at that time *peritrachelia* were also called *maniakia* – a term often found in 10th-century sources, especially in *De Cerimoniis*. There it refers to the golden collars worn by Imperial guards – a clear sign of rank, associated especially with the *Spathárokandidatoi*. The lack of references to them as armoured neck-protectors suggests that over time the *peritrachelion/ maniakion* lost an originally practical military function and developed into a simple sign of rank.

BELOW
A 9th–10th century *lorikion* of silvered ringmail, from Sofia. (Sofia Archaeological Museum; photo courtesy Prof Valeri Yotov)

Part of the breast area of a ringmail *lorikion* traditionally associated with the Byzantine general Leo Tornikios, *c.* AD 980; the riveted iron rings are 0.39in (1cm) in diameter, each passing through four others. Recent studies have confirmed the dating to the time of Basil II's wars, and traces of gold on some rings suggest that the armour was once completely gilded, which would support the belief that it belonged to a senior commander. (*in situ*, Iviron Monastery, Mt Athos)

Outer and inner surfaces of two *lamellae* from a 10th-century iron *klivanion* corselet from Vielki Preslav, Bulgaria. Note the central embossed ridges, and the attachment holes; the plates are shown here with the rounded ends upwards, typical of lamellar *klivania*. (Photo courtesy Prof Valeri Yotov)

The *Taktiká* of Leo VI and the *Sylloge Tacticorum* mention small tufts (*touphia mikra*) on top of helmets, presupposing the existence of fittings for a plume. The helmet could be held steady by a chin strap, and was worn over a padded head covering, probably of felt or quilted cloth – the 10th-century lexicon of Suidas mentions specifically a cap of thick felt (*pilios kentouklon*). The Byzantine army also used headgear made entirely of thick felt-like fabric, and also of leather. These *kamelaukia* served as a protection against the elements but could also be used in combat, especially by the lightly armed classes of soldiers. The *Liber de Ceremoniis* mentions, in relation to the soldiers of a warship, about 50 *epilorikia* ('over-mail armours') and 50 *kamelaukia*. The *Praecepta Militaria* describes *kamelaukia* of thick cloth, and says that they were held in place by a linen turban called a *phakeolion* wrapped around the head.

Body armour

The Taghmatics and Imperial Guards were given the best body protection available, and the *thorax*, *zava-lorikion* and *klivanion* are the main types of armours mentioned in the sources.

Thorax was the generic word for body protection, whether of scales, rings, or plain. For example, the *thorax lepidotos* mentioned in a 10th-century letter is an armour composed of small scales. The *thorax heroikon*, the old-fashioned muscled cuirass of Graeco-Roman tradition, was probably still in use in Byzantium at our period. Artistic representations show it worn by persons of the highest ranks, and a revival of such an armour might be linked to the predilection for ancient Roman military traditions seen during the Macedonian dynasty. While it was probably worn as parade armour, its use in battle cannot be excluded. In many representations – e.g. the Codex Esphigmenou 14 (folio 417v) – we see among heavy armoured cavalrymen some officers with muscled armour, worn in combination with ringmail or felt and leather protection. This was substantially a continuation of the tradition of the Late Antique cataphract, both Roman and Persian.

Such armour could be in leather with metal appliqués. It had transverse shoulder guards fastened with straps and attached to the breastplate by means of a button and ring. Long lappets or reinforcing strips of leather or metal (splint armour) are evident, and armours might have greater or lesser numbers of metal bosses, especially on the shoulders, upper arms and/ or belly. At this period metal decorative appliqués hinged to the lower border or *cymation* are rare. If an armour was entirely of leather, it had to be worked in such a way that this would not lose its hardened consistency. Sometimes muscled corselets were without any decoration, or had only shoulder pieces and a very stylized incision of the anatomical details (as visible on ivory caskets of the 10th–11th centuries).

The most mentioned and visible armour of the Guardsmen was the so-called *klivanion*, a lamellar or scale corselet usually made of interlocked iron, bronze, boiled leather or horn plates called *petala*. Normally the laced, unriveted lames of the early lamellar *klivanion* overlapped horizontally, from right to left. The lamellar rows were linked together by numerous thongs, and overlapped from the bottom upwards. The *klivanion* could be a long coat, but was usually a short corselet combined with padded garments and separate protection for the arms.

The Martyrdom of St Barbara, *c*. AD 1000. The archaic-looking muscled cuirass (*thorakion heroikon*), and the method of fastening the cloak across the chest, are reconstructed in Plate F2. (*Menologion* of Basil II, folio 224, Biblioteca Apostolica Vaticana, Rome; facsimile by Pio Franchi de Cavalieri, author's collection)

According to recent studies (by Dawson and Tsurtsumia) of artistic representations and the scarce but consistent archaeological finds, a new type of lamellar armour emerged in Byzantium from the end of the 10th century, becoming established in the 11th century. In this the plates did not overlap but were fixed to the leather base side by side. In representations of Guardsmen we find lamellar armours whose rows are separated by narrow bands; Dawson suggests that this was a leather band placed to separate the rows of lames and neutralize the 'scissors effect' caused by their movement, which might cut the thongs. Subsequently, such armours did not present these narrow bands, but wide leathers fully lining the plates. Later still, manufacture was further simplified by riveting the lames onto leather instead of fixing them together by means of thongs. The iconography distinguishes between so-called 'linear' and 'banded' armours; the former is frequently seen in the 10th century, perhaps even the 9th (an earlier example can be seen in the Kastoria frescoes), while the latter appears only in the 11th century. Essentially, the evolution of the *klivanion* in the 10th–11th centuries may be argued in three stages: (1) the introduction of a leather backing; (2) linear lamellar with double riveting; and (3), banded lamellar with riveting.

Many Guardsmen, members of the Imperial family and other high-ranking persons wore, on some occasions, *klivania* of gilded iron (*klivanion chryson*). For example, we read of the triumphal entry of Theophilus into Constantinople, when units of the Guard who had taken part in the Germanicea campaign against the Arabs accompanied the emperor into the city on horseback, all wearing gilded *klivania* and brandishing their swords and spears (*De Cer.*, I, 506).

The *lorikion* (also called *zava*) or ringmail armour was widely used by the Guardsmen; sometimes it was calf-length (Leo, *Tact.*, VI, 2), and worn in association with a buckled leather harness, and sometimes shorter. The surviving examples of Byzantine iron mail of the period – e.g., the fragment of the *lorikion* supposedly of the general Leo Tornikios preserved in the Iviron Monastery on Mt Athos, or the silvered specimen in Sofia Museum – show a ring construction identical to the Classical/ Late Roman style. Each ring passes through four other riveted rings; the ring diameter is 8–9mm, though 1cm (0.39in) in the Tornikios armour.

The *lorikion* was sometimes combined with a *klivanion* and worn under it for extra heavy protection. Round, concave shoulder protections (*mhela*) – made of metal or leather, and in the latter case sometimes covered with ringmail or scales – were attached to the main body armour (see illustration on page 16). These were sometimes decorated with small tufts or strips (*flamouliskia*) of different colours, probably regimental distinctions.

'Soft' armour

Strong garments of felt or quilted and padded fabric were worn instead of metal armours (*Syll. Tact.*, 38, 7) or under them, to protect the lower part of the body or the shoulders and upper arms. These included *kavadia*, which were padded armours made of coarse silk (*koukolion*) and cotton (*vamvakion*). Those of infantrymen were knee-length, fitted with wide sleeves called *manikia* that had slits in the internal side through which the arm could be slipped out to allow fuller freedom of movement. According to the *Praecepta Militaria* these slits began directly under the armpit, according to the *Sylloge Tacticorum* at the elbow. The open sleeves could be folded and fixed behind the shoulders with a button fastening.

Such garments are shown in Basil II's *Menologion* being worn by several Guard infantrymen.

In Leo VI's *Tactiká* (XIX, 13), marines are to be equipped with similar armours if *klivania* or *lorikia* are not available; here the term used is *nevrikà*, i.e. garments with a doubled padding of thick felt (*kentouklon*). In *Naumachica* (I, 14) we find fighting marines in *klivania* with scales only on the front part. In the list of equipment for the soldiers on each warship the *lorikia* are reserved to the officers or to soldiers with special equipment, and are notably fewer than the *klivania*, which were easier to make and cheaper than the ringmail shirts.

Arm protectors (*cheiromanika*, *cheiropsella*) were made of iron, wood, leather or padded fabric. The most common metal type were probably vambraces of splint construction, like those found in contemporaneous Khazar graves, but one-piece examples are also known. Similar leg pieces (*podopsella* or *chalkotouba*) are mentioned (Leo, IV, 34; *Syll. Tact.*, XXX, 2); these too might be of iron, wood or leather. A pair of greaves found at Gelendijk have been associated with those represented in Byzantine miniatures.

Over the armour, cavalrymen might wear a very loose-cut garment for protection against bad weather; this was called either an *epilorikion* ('over

A reconstruction drawing of an 11th-century fresco in Kiev, showing Basil II attended by *Protospathárioi* eunuchs wearing the white head-cloth; this *savana* could be brought around to cover the mouth when necessary. The Imperial shields and spears carried by the *Spathárioi*, *Protospathárioi*, *Kandidatoi* or *Protiktores* were kept inside the Sanctuary of St Theodore in the *Khrysotriklinos* throneroom of the Palace. In the fresco one shield is shown as enamelled gold and decorated with pearls, the other as a blue-green shade similarly decorated with gemstones. (St Sophia Museum, Kiev; author's photo, courtesy of the Museum)

11th-century Byzantine cavalry harness fittings. Among other items, this exceptional find from the Balkans includes: (top centre) the nose protector band of a snaffle bit, with squared strap dividers with a cut-out cross, in iron; (centre) a second example, with cruciform strap dividers, in iron, about 7.5in/ 19cm long; (centre right) a knobbed mace head of iron inlaid with silver, 2.3in/ 5.9cm high; (bottom left) a curb bit with extensions, in iron inlaid with silver, *c.* 8in/ 20.4cm long; and (bottom right) a U-shaped stirrup with chains, in iron inlaid with silver, 7.5in/ 19.1cm long. (Private collection; photo courtesy Gerhard Hirsch Nachfolger, Munich)

mail armour') or *epanoklivanion* ('over the *klivanion*'). The *Praecepta Militaria* (III, 4) advises such over-garments for *kataphraktoi*: 'over their *klivania* they should wear *epilorika* of cotton or coarse silk. Their hands should pass through the shoulder openings. Their sleeves should be left hanging behind the shoulders' (see reconstruction, Plate D3).

THE GEORGIAN CAMPAIGN, 1020

1: Emperor Basil II in full armour
This reconstruction of the 'Bulgar-Slayer', the most victorious emperor of the Macedonian dynasty, is taken from the Skilitzès miniatures (folio 195b), although reconstructed with archaeological artefacts of 11th-century date. Note the crown (*stemma*); the long *klivanion* made from large *lamellae* of gilded horn; the gilded scale arm defences – probably also made from some material lighter than iron; the splinted leg armour of gilded iron; and the shield with a gilded rim, decorated all over with precious stones. Behind him are arrayed a Varangian company, identifiable by their long-shafted battleaxes.

2: Standard-bearer of Imperial Tághmata
This standard-bearer of one of the Imperial cavalry regiments is armoured and accoutered according to the tactical manuals of the period; note the ringmail face protection, which was triple-layered. He is carrying a typical *vándon* banner, of squared shape with pointed streamers at the 'fly'. The cross or other Christian symbols were the normal charges of such standards.

3: Early Varangian *Archon*
This Russo-Scandinavian officer is based on recently cleaned frescoes from St Sophia in Kiev. Over a quilted defence for the neck he wears a helmet clearly descended from Late Roman models. His typical Byzantine armour incorporates scales and padded leather or fabric, and a white sash of rank can just be seen knotted characteristically high on the torso. Note his white *kampotouvia* boots, decorated with a typical motif – a feature apparently peculiar to the Varangians. In the foreground is a Georgian cross-standard, virtually indistinguishable from the East Roman type.

4: Abasgian armoured cavalryman
This messenger from the Georgian prince's army is taken from the Mravaldzali and Parakheti icons of the late 10th and early 11th centuries, and is essentially identical to his Byzantine counterparts. Yovhannes Draskhanakertc describes the host of Western Georgia (the Abkhazian or 'Abasgian' kingdom) in the 10th century as 'A numerous army, with steeds prancing in the air, the warriors wearing iron armour, formidable helmets, cuirasses with nail-studded iron plates [i.e. riveted *lamellae*] and sturdy shields, adornments, spears and swords'.

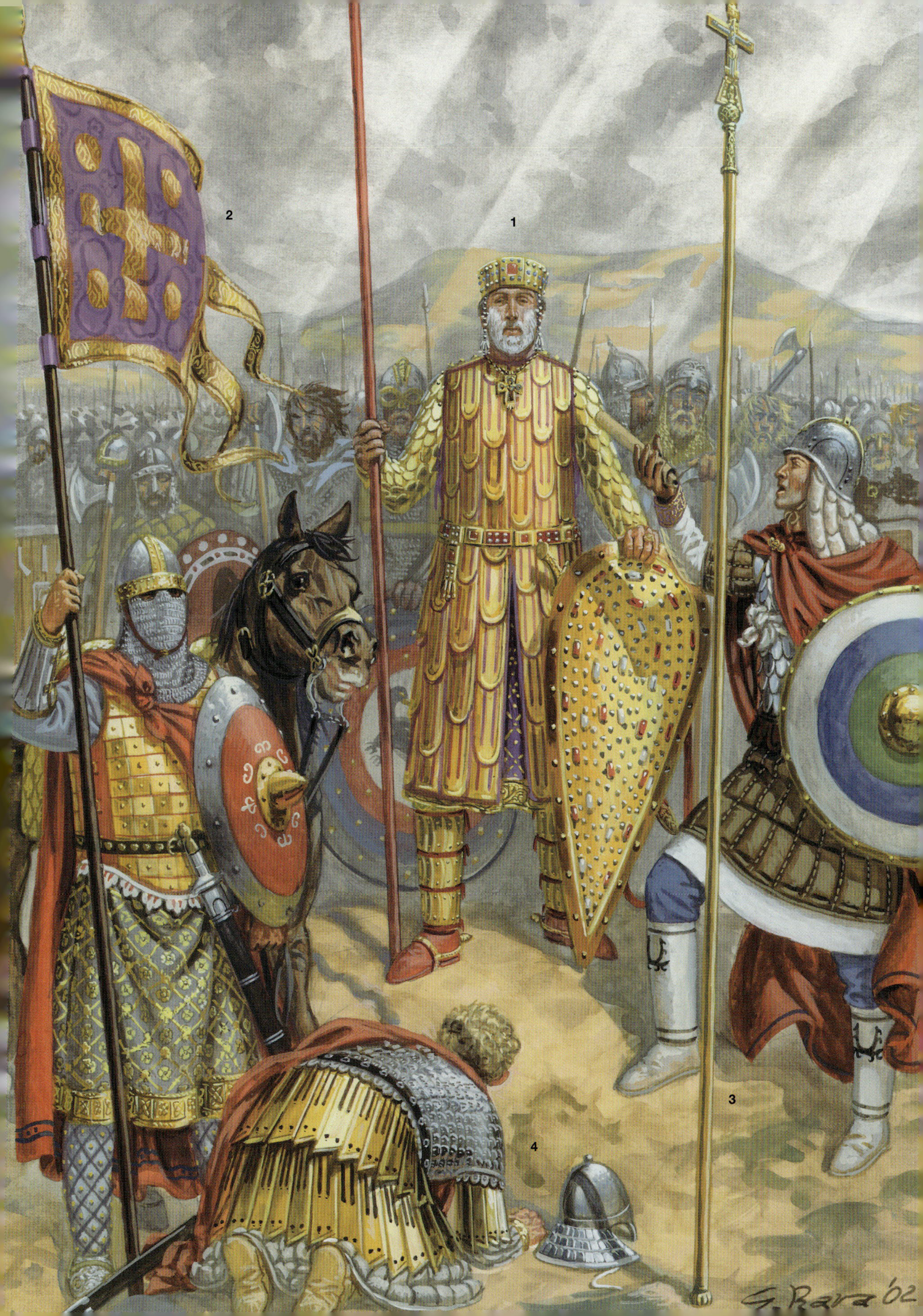
2
1
3
4
G. Rava '02

Shields

The shield (*skoutarion*, *thureos*, *aspis*) employed by the Guardsmen was usually of one of the standard types, but there were exceptions. Normally they were made of laminated wood covered with leather or parchment, framed with a metal, leather or rope edge, and reinforced with a central boss (*omphalos*, *boukolon*) and other metal fittings. A letter of the monk Maximos Planudes mentions the interesting detail that donkey-hide was often used to cover both shields and drums.

The shields might be kite-shaped, round, oval, or quadrilateral (a 'clipped kite' shape). The large oval shield that covered the man from face to ankles was employed in the great formations of infantrymen who formed battle arrays like the *foulkon*. According to the *Sylloge Tacticorum* and *Praecepta Militaria*, the heavy infantrymen should have either quadrilateral shields narrowing towards the bottom, about 6 spans high (55.25in/ 140.4cm); or three-cornered shields about the height of a man; or round shields about 3.5 spans (32.25in/ 82cm) in diameter. The *Sylloge* prescribes for the *kataphraktoi* shields 4.5 spans high (41.5in/ 105.3cm); the *Praecepta* specifies that cavalry shields should be shorter than those of the heavy infantry, so 4 or 5 spans high (c.37 or 46in/ 93.6 or 117 centimetres).

For court ceremonial and when in Constantinople the Guardsmen often carried round shields. The passage in *De Cerimoniis* describing the gear to be issued for a warship crew mentions 70 *skoutaria raptá* (sewn shields) and 30 *skoutaria lydiatika*. These terms probably refer respectively to leather shields and round polished bronze shields, like those used by the *Pámphyloi* elite sailors and the Macedonian soldiers of the Great *Etaireía*.

According to Leo VI's *Tactiká*, each unit should have shields painted in its own colour. The *Sylloge Tacticorum* speaks not only of a similar colour within each unit, but also an identical distinctive device. The costly parade shields of Imperial Guardsmen represented the apex of such decoration, being covered with gold and silver, and often decorated with pearls, like those represented in the hands of the *Protospathárioi* eunuchs in the frescoes of St Sofia in Kiev (see illustration on page 57).

Horse equipment

Eastern Roman cavalrymen are mentioned in the sources under the generic term of *kavallarioi*, but usually this word denotes the *kataphraktoi* – heavily armoured cavalrymen, sometimes mounted on fully or partly armoured horses. *De Ceremoniis* (81–82) mentions horse-armour in connection with the *Protospatharioi* eunuchs, *Spathárokandidatoi* and *Spatharioi*.

According to the *Sylloge* (31, 1), 'they protected the horses' heads with so-called brow-pieces (*prometopidiai*), and also the breasts and necks with small iron scales or plates'. The protection of the cataphracts' horses is mentioned by both Nikêphóros Phokás and Nikêphóros Ouranós: '[the *kataphraktoi*] must have sturdy horses covered in armour: either of pieces of felt and boiled leather fastened together down to the knees, so that nothing of the horse's body appears except its eyes and nostrils – likewise their legs below the knees and their undersides should remain uncovered and unconcealed; or they can have *klivania* made of buffalo-hide over the chest of the horse, divided at its legs and underneath to permit the unhindered movement of the legs'. Such horse-armour was not universal, but was usually fitted only to the mounts of those *kataphraktoi* who were employed in the triangular formation. This explains the rarity of artistic representations of armoured horses from our period; Taghmatic cavalrymen are usually shown riding unarmoured horses.

The horse furniture consisted of a head-piece (*kefalarea*), bridles (*klinkai*), and breast (*antilìna*) and rear (*postilìna, opisthelina*) straps both fixed to the padded structure of the saddle (*sella, sellochalinon*), which was furnished with stirrups (*skalai*). The harness was often decorated with disks or other appliqué metalwork. From the examination of original *phalerae* we can deduce that single straps were at least 1.3in (3.5cm) wide. The bit (*chalinarion, masshema*) used in the 10th–11th centuries derived from the Thracian iron type. The bridles were in interlaced leather, ending in a small loop for handling.

The saddle proper was of leather, raised, and sometimes furnished with wooden arches front and rear; it had a seat (*epìsellion*) of padded material, often coloured scarlet. This padded saddle was fastened by a girth. Below the saddle were double-layered leather flaps; the *antilìna* and *postilìna* passed over part of these and through two lateral holes in them, to attach to the saddle proper by means of buckles or buttons (*komposia*). Over all was a thick saddle cloth (*kapoulion*) of various colours, often purple or scarlet for the Imperial Guards.

Stirrups and spurs have been found in various excavations in Bulgaria. Iron horseshoes of the period have also come to light during excavations of the Danubian fortresses of Pacului Soare and Dinogetia-Garvan.

SELECT BIBLIOGRAPHY

Historical sources, and commentaries on same:
Anna Comnena, *Alexiadis*, ed. B.G. Niebuhr, 2 vols (Bonn, 1839)
Anonymus, *Theophanes Continuatus*, ed. I. Bekker (Weber, Bonn, 1838)
Codinus Curopalates, *De Officialibus Palatii Constantinopolitani, ex recognitione Immanuelis Bekkeri* (Bonn, 1839)
Constantinus Porphyrogenitus, *Tres tractatus de expeditionibus militaribus imperatoris* –'Three Treatises on Imperial military expeditions', ed. J.F. Haldon (Vienna, 1990)
Constantinus Porphyrogenitus, *De Cerimoniis Aulae Byzantinae libri duo*, ed. I.I. Reiske, 2 vols (Bonn, 1829 & 1830)
Constantinus Porphyrogenitus, *Le Livre des Cérémonies*, ed. A. Vogt, 2 vols (Paris, 1935)
Constantinus Porphyrogenitus, *De Administrando Imperio*, ed. G. Moravcsik & R.G.H. Jenkins (Washington DC, 1993)
Du Cange-Du Fresne, *Glossarium ad scriptores mediae et infimae graecitatis, duos in tomos digestum* (Lyon,1688)
Kedhrenos G., *Georgius Cedrenus, Johanni Scylitzae Ope ab I. Bekkero suppletus et emendatus, Synopsis Historiarum*, tomus alter (Bonn, 1839)
Laurent, V., *Les Corpus de sceaux de l'Empire byzantin, II, L'Administration centrale* (Paris, 1981)
Leo Diaconus, *Leonis Diaconis Caloensis Historiae libri decem*, ed. C.B. Hase-Weber (Bonn, 1828)
Leonis Imperatoris Tactica, ed. Meursius-Lamius, Migne, in *Patrologia Graeca Cursus Completus*, vol. CVII, col. 668–1094
Naumachica, ed. A. Dain (Paris, 1943)
'Praecepta Militaria of Nikêphóros Phokas and Tactica of Nikêphóros Ouranós' in McGeer, E., 1995, *Sowing the Dragon's Teeth: Byzantine Warfare in the 10th Century* (Washington, pp. 3–171)

Heavy 10th–11th century Byzantine stirrup from the Varna region of Bulgaria; the rich inlaid decoration of this splendid piece shows strong Iranian or Turkic influence. Turkish, Khazar and Arab warriors were all serving with the Imperial armies during this period, and their styles are found reflected in Byzantine weaponry and equipment. (Photos courtesy Prof Valeri Yotov)

Sylloge Tacticorum, quae olim 'Inedita Leonis Tactica' dicebatur, ed. A. Dain (Paris,1938)

Three Byzantine Military Treatises, ed. G.T. Dennis (Washington, 1985)

Some modern works:

D'Amato, R., 'A Prôtospatharios, Magistros, and Strategos Autokrator of 11th cent.: the equipment of Georgios Maniakes and his army according to the Skylitzes Matritensis miniatures and other artistic sources of the middle Byzantine period', in *Porphyra*, Supplement 4

D'Amato, R., *The Varangian Guard 988–1453* (Osprey, Oxford, 2010)

Dawson, T., 'Kremasmata, Kabadion, Klibanion: some aspects of middle Byzantine military equipment reconsidered', in *Byzantine and Modern Greek Studies* 22 (1958)

Dawson, T., 'Suntagma Oplon, The equipment of regular Byzantine troops, *c.* 950 to *c.* 1204', in D.Nicolle, *A Companion to Medieval Arms and Armour* (London, 2002)

Haldon, J.F., *Byzantine Praetorians* (Bonn, 1984)

Haldon, J.F., 'Some aspects of the Byzantine military technology from the Sixth to the Tenth Centuries', in *Byzantine and Modern Greek Studies* 1 (1975)

Heath, I., *Byzantine Armies 886–1118* (Osprey, London, 1979)

Heath, I., *Armies of the Dark Ages 600–1066* (Worthing, 1980)

Hoffmeyer, A.B., 'Military Equipment in the Byzantine Manuscript of Skylitzes in Biblioteca Nacional in Madrid', in *Gladius 5* (Granada, 1966)

Kolias, T.G., *Byzantinische Waffen* (Vienna, 1988)

Nicolle, D., *Medieval Warfare Source Book, Volume 2: Christian Europe and its Neighbours* (London, 1996)

Nicolle, D., *Romano-Byzantine Armies, 4th–9th Centuries* (London, 1992)

Schlumberger, G., *Sigillographie de l'Empire Byzantin* (Paris, 1884, r/p Turin, 1963)

Schlumberger, G., *Un Empereur byzantin au dixième siècle* (Paris, 1890)

Schlumberger, G., *L'epopéè byzantine à la fin du dixième siècle*, 2 vols (Paris, 1896 & 1900)

Schreiner, P., 'Zur Ausrustung des Kriegers in Byzanz, dem Kiever Russland und Nordeuropa nach bildlichen und literarischen Quellen', in *Les Pays du Nord et Byzance (Skandinavie et Byzance), Actes du colloque nordique et international de byzantinologie tenu à Upsal 20–22 avril 1979* (Upsala, 1981)

Tsurtsumia, M., 'The Evolution of Splint Armour in Georgia and Byzantium: Lamellar and Scale Armour in the 10th–12th Centuries', in *Byzantina Symmeikta*, 21 (2011)

Yotov, V., 'About the Byzantine Swords (5th–11th centuries): Problems of their Typology', paper presented in *Nis and Byzantium IX 'Towards the celebration of the anniversary of the Edict of Milan'* (Nis, 2010)

INDEX

References to illustrations and plates are shown in **bold**. Captions to plates are shown in brackets.

Abasgian army **59** (58)
administration 4, 14, 16, 29
Anatolia 4, 9, 10
Anonymus de re militari 16, 24, 32
Arabs *see* Islamic world
archaeology 40–1, 43, 45, 48, 52, 56
archery 49, **51**
Armenia 16

banners *see* flags
Basil I 4, 30, 45
Basil II Porphyrogenitus 5, 9, 10, 11, 14, 30, **38**, 39, 57, **59** (58)
Bithynia 13
Blues (imperial colour) 24, 25, 27, 40, **42** (43)
bodyguards 29, 30, 31, 37, 38
Boukoleon Harbour 28, 32, **47** (46)
Bulgaria 13, 14, 29, 40
Bulgarian Siege (913) **12** (13)

Christianity 31
clothing 4, 5, 9, 10, **11**, **12** (13), **14**, **16**, **17**, **18**, **19** (18), **21**, **26** (27), 27, **31**, **33**, **34**, **35** (34), 37, **38**, 39–40, **42** (43), **47** (46); *see also* defensive equipment: body armour; helmets; 'soft' armour
commanders 15–16, 20, 22, 23, 24, 25, 27, 36, 37; naval 28–9, 32–3
commodores 29
Constantine I the Great 14
Constantine V 14, 15, 17, 20, 21, 25, 37
Constantine VII Porphyrogenitus 5, 6, 7, **27**, 28, 32
Constantine X Dukas 32
Constantinople 4, 6, 11, 13, 14, 20, 22, 24; defence of 24–5, 27, 28–9
Crete expeditions 6, 15, 28, 33, 38, 41

Dalmatians 32, 33
ad-Dawla, Emir Saif 6, 7, 14
defensive equipment: body armour **12** (13), **13**, **19** (18), **47** (46), 55–6, **59** (58); helmets 7, 51–5; scabbards 9, 10, **11**, **18**, 41; shields 4, 5, **11**, **14**, **18**, **19** (18), **21**, **22**, **26** (27), **31**, 57, 60; 'soft' armour 56–8

escorts 20, 25, 32, 36, 37
eunuchs 27, 36–7, 57

fighters 23, 28, 38–9
flags 21, 23, 25, 29–30, 30, 33, 46
foreigners 23, 28, 29, 31, 32
Franks 31

Georgian Campaign (1020) **59** (58)
Great Palace *see* Sacred Palace
'Greek Fire' 6, 32, 53
Greens (imperial colour) 24, 25, 27, 40

Heraclius 10
Hippodrome (Constantinople) 22, 23, 32, 36, 37, 49
horse equipment **12** (13), **15**, **42** (43), 58, 60–1, **62**
Hungarians 7, 31
hunting 30, 36, **42** (43), 45

iconography 41, 45, 48, 56
Imperial Guardsmen 4, 5, **11**, **19** (18), **22**, **33**, 43–4, **50** (51); *Archontogennhematai* 38; *Maghlavítai* **19** (18), 30, 34, 36; *Sardoi* 38–9; *Teichistai* 14; *Vasilikê Etaireía* **19** (18), **21**, 30–2; *Vasilikodhrómonion* 32–3; *Vasilikoi Anthropoi* **19** (18), 36–8
Imperial navy 27–30, 31, 32–3, 44, **47** (46), 57
Iohannes Dzimiskés 5, 7, 9, 24, **42** (43), 44, 49
Irene, Empress 22, 34
Islamic world 4–5, 11, 13, 29, 31
Italian expedition (935) 38

John Protospathários 28
Joshua 10, **11**, **38**, **39**
Julian the Apostate **31**
junior officers 17, 20

Khazars 31, 57
Kletorologion 15, 20, 29, 37

legal matters 29, **30**
Lemnos 29
Leo I 20, 25, 28
Leo the Diacon 24, 44, 49
Leo VI the Wise 5, 15, 20, 29, 32, 37, 45, 57, 60
Leo XI 20
Liber de Ceremoniis 16, 17, 20, 22, 24, 25, 27, 31, 38

Macedonia 4, 13, 15, 20, 30, 31, 32, 55
Marianos Argyros 7, 31
Menologion 43, 45, 46, 57
messengers 20, 22, 23, 24, 36
Michael II 24
Michael III 39
military operations 14, 11, 15, 27
military personnel 11, **12** (13), 13, 14, 15–17, 20, 20–3, 23, 24, 25, 27
Moors 31
musicians 30

naval expeditions 27
Nikêphóros I 22, 23
Nikêphóros II Phokás 5, 7, 15, 31, 32, **35** (34), **42** (43), 45, 49, 60
Nikêphóros Ouranós 14, 49, 60
Notitia Dignitatum 14, 16

Persia 29
Philippopolis 24
physical appearance 37, 38

police duties 23, 25, 34, 36
Praecepta Militaria 15, 48
prisons 24, 25
provinces *see Thémata*

Reds (imperial colour) 24, 25, 27, 40
Rhomanós I Lecapênós 5, 15, 16, 28, 32, 36, 38
Rus, the 6, 31, 32, 33
Russia 29
Russo-Scandinavians 4, 39

Sacred Palace **17**, 21, 22, 23, 24, 30, 36, 37, 52; ceremonies at **26** (27), 32
Saracens 31
sheath-bearers 36
ships 27–8, 30, 32–3, **47** (46)
Simeon I of Bulgaria 4, 5, 6
sport 22
St Barbara 55
St George 34
St Gregory of Nazianzius 23
St Helen 27
St Porphyrius 33
St Theodore Stratilates 14
St Theodosius 23
standard-bearers 16–17, 20–1, 23, 24, 25, 29–30, **59** (58)
Svyátoslav, Prince of Kiev 7, 24
sword-bearers 37
Sylloge Tacticorum 15, 45, 46, 49, 54, 56, 60

Tághmata regiments 5, 10, **11**, 13–14, 37; *Athanatoi* 14, 24, **42** (43); *Eskoubitores* 20–3, 25, 27; *Exkoúvitoi* 14; *Ikanátoi* 14, 23–4; *Noúmeroi* 14, 24–5, 27; *Skhólai* **12** (13), 14–17, 20, 25; *Teichistai* 24–5, 27; *Vighla (Arithmós)* 14, 22–3, 30, 32; *see also Vasilikoploimon*
Taktika 20, 29, 57, 60
Taktikón 16, 20, 24, 31
Thémata 10–11, 13, 22
Theodosius III 37
Theophilos 25, 56
Thessaloniki 29
Thrace 4, 13, 15, 20
Turkey 31, 40

Varangian Guards 38, 39, **59** (58)
Várdhas Phokás 6, 9, 31, 39
Vasiléfs (emperor) 13, 30, 32, 36, 38; *see also* individual emperors
Vasilikoploimon 14, 27–30
Vasilios *Parakoimomenos* 28, 29, 52
vice-commanders 15, 25, 36, 37
Vita Ioannici 20
Vladimir, Grand Prince of Kiev 39

weapons: axes 39, 48–9; bows 49; clubs 36; daggers 45; maces 34, 46, 48; spears **21**, 46; swords 5, 6, **12** (13), **18**, **19** (18), **23**, **26** (27), **27**, 34, 37, 41, 43–4; war-hammers 49
Whites (imperial colour) 24, 25, 27, 40